Mrs. Sigourney of Hartford

Mrs. Sigourney of Hartford

Poems and Prose on the Early American Deaf Community

EDNA EDITH SAYERS AND DIANA MOORE

EDITORS

Gallaudet University Press
Washington, D.C.

Gallaudet University Press
Washington, DC 20002
http://gupress.gallaudet.edu

Cover photo credits
Portrait of Lydia Sigourney: Library of Congress, Prints & Photographs Division,
LC-BH82-5220 A
American School for the Deaf: Library of Congress, Prints & Photographs
Division, LC-DIG-pga-01650

Library of Congress Cataloging-in-Publication Data

Mrs. Sigourney of Hartford : poems and prose on the early American deaf
community / Edna Edith Sayers and Diana Moore, editors.

  p. cm.

  ISBN 978-1-56368-557-6 (pbk.) — ISBN 978-1-56368-558-3 (e-book)

  1. People with disabilities—Literary collections. 2. Sigourney, L. H.
(Lydia Howard), 1791–1865—Criticism and interpretation. I. Sayers, Edna
Edith, 1951–. II. Moore, Diana, 1952–
  PS2831.S29 2013
  811'.3—dc23   2012045490

For
William Sayers
and
Michael L. Moore

Contents

Acknowledgments

We are most grateful to Harlan Lane, who generously gave us a complete copy of the notes and sources on Lydia Sigourney that he had gathered over the years, beginning with his earliest work toward *When the Mind Hears,* but which had never found their way into any of his publications. Thanks, Harlan! Gary Wait, Archivist at the American School for the Deaf in West Hartford, likewise generously shared with us information he had gathered on Sigourney and on Julia Brace but had not (yet) used in the preparation of any publication. Gary also has promptly and cheerfully answered odd questions from us over many years. Judy Yaeger Jones kindly provided information about Sigourney's correspondence with Laura Redden.

The following Connecticut libraries were most helpful and very kind to us, two Deaf women from Washington, D.C., who must have appeared rather stunned by the wealth of archival material to be seen seemingly everywhere, just for the asking: the Stowe-Day Library at the Harriet Beecher Stowe Center in Hartford, which holds a surprisingly large selection of editions of various Sigourney books not readily available elsewhere; the Connecticut Historical Society, which most kindly let us in to work on a day when they had planned to be closed for renovations; the Hartford Public Library, where we were able to sample the Hartford Courant's stories on the new Asylum and the doings of Dr. Cogswell, Mrs. Sigourney, and just about everyone connected with the early years of the Asylum; the Watkinson Library and College Archives of Trinity College, Hartford, which holds some unexpected material on Thomas Hopkins Gallaudet's life outside of the Asylum; and finally, at Yale, the Beinecke Rare Book and Manuscripts Library, the Sterling Memorial Library's Manuscripts and Archives collection, and the Medical History Library, which hold, respectively, many rare editions of Sigourney's books, the Cogswell Family Papers, and material relating to Dr. Cogswell's medical career. We thank the Gallaudet Research Institute for travel grants that made research at these libraries possible, and Don Reid of Butternut Farm, Glaston-bury, for his hospitality and geese eggs. In Maryland and Wash-ington, D.C., the Gallaudet University Library Deaf Collections and Archives, the Johns Hopkins University Milton S. Eisenhower Library, and the University of Maryland's Maryland Room at the Hornbake Library North all very kindly assisted our research, the last even opening up an exhibit case to remove a book so that we could consult it on the spot.

Many thanks to Susannah Macready for reading a draft of the introduction and suggesting improvements.

Introduction

Lydia Howard Huntley Sigourney (1791–1865) of Hartford, Connecticut, was an internationally known poet in her day, the author of fifty-six books, some of which ran up to twenty editions; a contributor of countless poems, prose sketches, and some two thousand articles to magazines; and a supporter of nearly every progressive cause known to the age, including deaf education, a new idea in antebellum America. Today, not only the poems she wrote but also her role in American progressive activism are all but forgotten. Sigourney (pronounced "SIG er nee") is sometimes remembered in Deaf history as the first teacher of Alice Cogswell, the deaf girl whose father spearheaded the founding of the oldest continuing school for the deaf in North America, although she appears even in this field as a shadowy figure behind Deaf history's heroes Thomas Hopkins Gallaudet and Laurent Clerc. In reality, she taught Alice reading, writing, history, geography, and arithmetic using some sort of signed language, now irrecoverable, before Clerc, and perhaps even Gallaudet, ever met the child, and certainly before any Deaf community began to emerge in Hartford around the school they would found. How all this came to happen, and how Sigourney continued the friendships she made in Deaf Hartford for the rest of her life, are stories related a bit further on in this introduction.

As for her other progressive causes, which, unfortunately, we have space here only to sketch, she was perhaps not as well synchronized with the times or as well aligned with history's winners. For example, she believed fervently in education for girls and detested both ornamental needlework and corsets, but by 1848, when Elizabeth Cady Stanton drafted the Declaration of Sentiments in Seneca Falls, New York, Sigourney was too old to grasp the need for women to vote. She was an abolitionist, but she poured her energies into what now seems a quixotic endeavor: establishing libraries for the few black Americans who were settling in Liberia. Hartford was generally conservative on abolition until the 1850s, and Sigourney's focus on emigration was typical of the antislavery views of the city.[1] It's interesting to note, however, that unlike many other Hartford antislavery advocates, such as Thomas Hopkins Gallaudet, who staked his black servant her passage to Liberia, Sigourney actually had friendly, peer relationships with at least one African American who decided to emigrate: Augustus Washington, the Hartford daguerreotypist who had attended Dartmouth College and later wrote chatty, informal letters to Sigourney about his Liberian sugar farm.

In other endeavors—advocacy for disabled veterans, Irish immigrants (though not their religion), the elderly, American Indians, and prisoners—Sigourney was so far ahead of her time that history has not yet spotted her efforts. Of course, much of this work could be characterized as personal kindness. For example, Sigourney's friend and fellow educator Catharine Beecher tells the story of a man sentenced to prison for stealing some of Sigourney's jewelry. While he was incarcerated, Sigourney "so ministered to both his spiritual and temporal wants" that, when he was released, he came to visit her, saying that "her kindness had changed his character."[2] In other cases, we see real activism. Her advocacy for Indians, for example, included the 4,000-line narrative poem "Traits of the Aborigines of America" (1822), which took the Indian point of view and asserted that the hostility was created by whites, and "A Legend of Pennsylvania" (1846), which called for white, female pacifism to stop further massacre of Indians. Half the chapters of her *Sketch of Connecticut* (1824) were devoted to the Mohegans. And along with Catharine Beecher, she organized a national women's petition campaign against Andrew Jackson's 1830 Indian Removal Act. All this and more in an era when American society was complacently anti-Indian. None of her work actually influenced U.S. Indian policy, however, and by the time attitudes and laws began to change in the mid-twentieth century, Sigourney's work was long forgotten. In her day, her writings were praised for their "grand moral tendency" and "philanthropic zeal" and were received as evidence that "the one great aim of her soul, is—*to do good*," and that was the ultimate compliment.[3]

In the case of her poems and prose sketches, that they are forgotten today is perhaps less surprising. Known to contemporaries as the "Sweet Singer of Hartford," Mrs. Sigourney, as she signed her published work, belonged to the vast nineteenth-century literary movement called sentimentalism, which produced a type of literature not greatly appreciated today by cultivated readers, although it still thrives in film and popular music as well as in advertising and fund-raising appeals. And she was most famous for her obituary poems, a genre associated today only with amateur efforts in small-town weeklies. Nevertheless, as we shall see, her poems and prose sketches were of a piece with her social activism and a means by which, in the words of Mark David Hall, she "actively promulgated a well thought out vision of society and politics."[4]

The Sentimental Tradition*

When we describe a novel or film as "sentimental" today, what we usually mean is that it is insincerely or manipulatively emotional. We don't like to feel that we've been manipulated and, what's more, we associate sentimentality with appeals to pull out our checkbooks, both in advertising ("A diamond is forever") and the big business of charity ("Look at me, I'm walking!"). To understand poems and prose sketches in the sentimental tradition by Sigourney and other American women writers of her generation, one must get back to what sentimentality meant during the formative years of these poets, the early nineteenth century, when sentimentalists were writers with agendas—progressive agendas. Recent studies

---

*This section on sentimentalism and the next on women writers and women's magazines present synopses of scholarship, mostly from the last thirty years, which broke new ground in giving serious academic attention to writers and genres previously ignored by literary history and criticism. The work of Ann Douglas (who also published on Sigourney as Ann Douglas Wood), Jane Tompkins, and Joanne Dobson ground our synopses. Other scholars whose work was consulted for these synopses are Nina Baym, Max Cavitch, Betty Harris Day, Judith Fetterly, Annie Finch, Philip Fisher, Allison Giffen, Elizabeth Gitter, Mark David Hall, Mary Hershberger, Jerome McGann, Patricia Okker, Alicia Suskin Ostriker, Fred Lewis Patee, Elizabeth Petrino, Sarah Robbins, Melissa Teed, Cheryl Walker, Joyce W. Warren, Emily Stipes Watts, and Sandra Zagarell.

have only now begun to show that beneath the surface of Sigourney's sentimentalism, and the sentimentalism of antebellum women writers in general, lies a rebel in conservative clothing, as a recent doctoral dissertation has it.[5]

Sentimentalism—or, rather, its precursor, sensibility—first appeared near the end of the eighteenth century as a reaction against neoclassicism, which, as exemplified in English literature by the poetry of Alexander Pope and the prose of Samuel Johnson, had held that reason must dominate emotion and imagination. Sensibility, in contrast, declared feelings superior to reason, and a better guide to the moral life. Sensibility was thus an aspect of the Romantic movement and played a role in the political revolutions of the era (as has been shown most recently by Sarah Knott's study of how sensibility informed and enabled the American Revolution) and, later, social reform movements such as abolition. In literature, male poets like Wordsworth and Byron were to pull Romanticism into an obsession with the *individual's* feelings, while sentimentalism, increasingly the sphere of the female writer and reader, in contrast explored feelings for their value to the community. This distinction between a male focus on the individual and a female focus on the community is a key difference for any study of women's literature of the American antebellum period, and one we return to below.

The rise of American sentimentalism (and Romanticism) in literature at the beginning of the nineteenth century paralleled a similar shift in American religion, where new evangelical movements like Methodism embraced emotional modes of knowing Jesus, in contrast to the older, established, state-sponsored Calvinist churches that continued to focus on doctrine and prescribed forms of worship. During this so-called Second Great Awakening, church membership soared as people flocked to the new Methodist and Baptist congregations, where evangelical Christianity and the sentimentalism it fostered broke through entrenched notions that the moral life was something one learned from an authoritative figure or church-endorsed interpretation of scripture. Now, right living could be discovered in one's own heart. American sentimentalist novels and poems of the antebellum period were informed by their authors' heartfelt views that Jesus calls upon each of us to be loving and charitable. Jesus also provided these writers with the "higher authority" they needed to buck uncharitable social mores and unjust laws such as the 1850 Fugitive Slave Act. We must keep in mind, as well, that deaf education itself was founded for the express purpose of bringing "the happiness of religious truth" to the deaf, as Sigourney reminds us in her *Memoir of Phebe P. Hammond*, reprinted here.

So, while the Bible is certainly, as Gary Kelly phrased it, a "ubiquitous presence in her work,"[6] as are more general references to popular Christian beliefs like heavenly harps and so on, Sigourney's writing was well within the normal range for its time. We can see such religiosity in her pupil Alice's early letters, which are full of expressions like "I pray morning and evening,–God to keep Alice and all men" (in Alice's letter, further excerpted on p. 25), in little Phebe Hammond's study of the dictionary and the catechism as though they were two books of equal importance to her education (in *Memoir*, reprinted in part 2), in titles of T. H. Gallaudet's books, like *The Child's Book on Repentance*, and so on.

While sentimentality maintained its links with evangelical Christianity and with progressive social reform, its literature played out mostly in the secular world of home and family life. Sentimentality's valorization of feeling over intellect often appears in literature as a domestic battle with rationality, as, for example, in Mary Shelley's 1818 *Frankenstein*, where the rational scientist Victor Frankenstein creates an emotional monster who ruins his creator's life in a desperate search for familial love and domestic belonging. In the United States, sentimental literature celebrated the nuclear family, which was fast replacing the large eighteenth-century household comprising not only blood relatives of various degrees and generations, but also hired hands, apprentices, and servants. The nuclear family was thus another key concept underpinning Sigourney's work and that of other American sentimentalists, as it still today underpins many advertising campaigns.

While sentimentalism thus privileges emotions and community, and coincides with evangelical religious practices and the valorization of the nuclear family, a sentimental work can also be recognized by internal characteristics. To modern eyes, a sentimental work is long—very long. This is so not because there is anything complex to be conveyed, but rather, according to Northrup Frye, because emotion is being "maintained at a continuous present by various devices of repetition."[7] A poem like the twenty-eight-stanza "On Seeing the Deaf, Dumb, and Blind Girl of the American Asylum, Hartford, at a Festival" will thus seem overlong and repetitive to us. Unlike many of her contemporaries, however, Sigourney could write short poems, too, and some of these are among her best.

The essential mark of the sentimental work is its premise that human relationships based on familial affection (rather than erotic love) are the goal of every life. Mothers and their children are usually the topic, although affection between siblings or friends, a teacher and her pupils, or a grandparent and child may also be featured, and these personal bonds are projected outward into the celebration of the communal spirit and sympathy with others in general, a projection that can be seen quite clearly in many of Sigourney's poems.

The plot of a sentimental narrative develops out of a threat to a familial, affectional, or communal bond, or an actual breaking of a bond that must somehow be restored. In Harriet Beecher Stowe's 1852 *Uncle Tom's Cabin*, when Tom is sold away from his family and Eliza is threatened with the sale of her young son, their familial and affectional bonds are in danger of being broken, and the plot is off and running. For sentimentalists, the evils of slavery lay not in its theft of labor, but rather in its destabilization of the nuclear family, when the sale of human beings separated husbands from wives, mothers from children.

The primacy of family and affectional relationships in sentimentalist literature is easiest to see if we place a novel like *Uncle Tom's Cabin* against contemporary American Romantic or Transcendentalist narratives like Henry David Thoreau's 1854 *Walden* or Herman Melville's 1851 *Moby-Dick*. In *Walden*, Thoreau describes his experiment in isolating himself from society and his enjoyment of the resultant complete self-reliance. In *Moby-Dick*, Ishmael happily leaves home under his own volition to seek his fortune, and he forms no further significant human ties, preferring the role of detached observer. That the works of male Romantics like Melville and Thoreau are more likely to be regarded as "great books" today than are sentimentalist works of women authors suggests why many of us are embarrassed to say we enjoy reading Harriet Beecher Stowe's story of people seeking—not running away from—affection and domesticity.

Death, the ultimate breach of human relationships, was naturally a major topic not only of the sentimental novel but also of lyric poetry in the sentimental tradition, and here we come to the obituary poems for which Sigourney was so famous in her own day. The elegy, a formal lament over a death, had been continuously popular in America since the earliest English settlements, but by the nineteenth century, although almost every poet wrote at least a few of these poems, most elegies were being composed by women. And the subgenre of the infant or child elegy was at its height. Childhood death was rampant in the nineteenth century, with more than half of all births ending in death before adolescence, and these deaths, whether during birth or from accidents or infectious diseases, took place at home, where the women of the household tended the dying child and prepared its body for viewing and burial. One would expect to see highly personal elegies composed by mothers, but instead we find that even infant elegies are remarkable for their public, rather than personal, outlook. Far from being meditations on the poet's own loss, even the infant elegies of women poets reach out to all the grieving survivors and the larger community, a feature quite marked in Sigourney's obituary poems, including those reprinted here on her old friends Thomas Hopkins Gallaudet ("Hymn"), Alice's father ("Funeral of Dr. Mason F. Coggswell"), and Alice herself. This feature, in fact, may account for some of our puzzlement in reading Sigourney's poems today. Trained as we are on the (male) Romantics, from whom we have learned to expect a well-defined poetic voice, we search for a voice, an "I," in these poems, but in vain.

As probably might have been expected, the obituary poem and its mostly female authorship were commonly disparaged by male writers, even in the early Victorian era that was its heyday and Sigourney's prime of life. In the *Adventures of Huckleberry Finn*, set in the 1830s, Emmeline Grangerford is a poetess so prolific with her lachrymose elegies that when someone was ill, we read in chapter 17, "it was the doctor first, then Emmeline, then the undertaker." Actually, such mockery of the elegiac poem composed by a woman goes back at least as far as 1722, when Benjamin Franklin's "Silence Dogood" gave readers a "receipt," or recipe, "to make a "New-England funeral Elegy": "add his last Words, dying Expressions, &c. if they are to be had; mix all these together and be sure you strain them well. Then season all with a handful or two of Melancholly Expressions," and so on.[8] Sigourney's obituary poems were mocked by men ranging from the president of Yale College in the 1880s and 1890s to her twentieth-century biographer Gordon Haight. This apparent need to denigrate the genre perhaps merits a study of its own.

There is no denying that the child elegy could be, and often was, clichéd—Silence Dogood's recipe is a witty reminder of just how formulaic the elegy could be. The dying child is always passive and accepting, a model for adults in how to achieve a "good death"; the survivors are certain that the child is in heaven and they look forward to reunion there; and the child's early death "casts an aura of holiness and spiritual precocity over his life,"[9] a feature observable in Sigourney's *Memoir of Phebe P. Hammond*. Sigourney's additions to the established formula, as we shall see in the obituary poems included in this volume, include the idea that mourning should displace other social demands on survivors and a focus on those survivors that acknowledges their individual experiences of the loss.

Outside the obituary poem, where the main character is already dead and the survivors' affectional bonds already broken, at least until the hoped-for heavenly reunion where "the fearful word *to part* / Is never breathed" (as Sigourney puts it in "Alice"), the subject matter of human relationship and its vulnerability to threat dictates that the protagonist of a sentimental story must be a defenseless figure whose bonds with loved ones can easily be broken, but who is wholly innocent of causing her own misfortune, which arrives without explanation. Such a character need not, and commonly does not, have the intellect, education, or sophistication to cogitate on her situation. Popular choices, therefore, included destitute widows and orphans, the frail elderly, people with various disabilities, "primitive" peoples, slaves, and so on.

The deaf boy or girl who was attending the newly founded Connecticut Asylum for the Education and Instruction of Deaf and Dumb Persons in Hartford was perfect for this role: she is innocent, any affectional bonds she may have with her family back home, with whom she does not share a spoken language, are extremely tenuous and highly vulnerable to threat, and it is easy to portray her as unable to understand her plight. It is important to note here that, outside of the languageless deaf-blind woman Julia Brace, Sigourney never presented a deaf adult in this role. For one thing, the deaf adults Sigourney knew were far too intelligent, sophisticated, and well educated to function as focuses for sentimental poems, and they certainly were not marginalized figures in Hartford. Also, deaf education was a significant item in Sigourney's progressive agenda: readers who come to pity the deaf schoolgirl will then subscribe to the establishment of a school for her, as Mr. and Mrs. Charles Sigourney subscribed to the Hartford school. In fact, magazines that published any kind of story about the school almost invariably presented it as evidence of "the power of education," making an implicit argument for taxpayer support of these schools.[10] It is also well to keep in mind that while early pupils sometimes had deaf siblings, few had deaf parents, so the typical entering pupil was truly an abject figure, having been deprived of language in any form until her arrival at the Hartford school.

These notions about the abject deaf—and deaf-blind—child are easily illustrated by a twentieth-century play and film, *The Miracle Worker*, which fits pretty squarely in the antebellum sentimental tradition: it depicts little Helen Keller's misfortune to have been random ill luck for which no one is to blame, and the consequence of this misfortune to be isolation from her family and alienation from its affection, as is indicated when her father is annoyed by her and her older brother mocks her as a monkey. Without affectional bonds, she is wholly abject and scarcely human: bad tempered, violent, selfish, and very, very dirty. The three-hanky ending at the water pump, where she suddenly understands that the fingerspelling protocol forced on her by Anne Sullivan is in fact language, delivers Helen to her rightful place in the affectionate family circle. This happy ending is very different from what an imagined nonsentimentalist playwright might have chosen: such a writer might see the water-pump scene as the key not to Helen's restoration to familial affection, but rather to her literacy, college degree, and rewarding adult life of international political activism.

Actually, *The Miracle Worker*'s use of language acquisition as a means of restoring Helen to her family circle marks it as a twentieth-century knock-off, not an authentic work of the sentimentalist tradition. The sentimentalists, like the Romantics, viewed spoken language as an aspect of the postlapsarian world, a result of our

alienation from God—or Nature. Wordsworth, for example, frequently writes of spiritual knowledge and understanding that need
no sound or voice, while Stowe creates characters who signal their
redemption by touches and tears, rather than words. While many of
the Romantics' mute or inarticulate characters were male (as were
some of Stowe's), in general, as Elizabeth Gitter has written, the
sentimentalists' "celebration of speechlessness narrowed into a more
limited glorification of the inarticulate heroine and into an identifi-
cation of silence with a spiritualized femininity."[11]

Gitter cites the heroines of a male sentimentalist, Charles Dickens,
such as Little Nell and Lucy Manette, as examples of the sentimental
heroine "too fragile, unworldly, or innocent to use her tongue." In
the real world, this literary conjunction of innocence and muteness
was put to work raising funds for the Perkins Institution for the
Blind in Boston, when in 1837 its director, Samuel Gridley Howe,
brought deaf-blind Laura Bridgman to the school and groomed her
to be "perfectly and innately good," "cheerful, reverent, and unself-
ish," to remind the public of "the helpless, suffering little heroines
of sentimental literature."[12]

Howe was an opportunist; the deaf school that Gallaudet, Clerc,
and Hartford's leading citizens founded, and that Mrs. Sigourney
supported all her life, did not exploit their own deaf-blind female
pupil, Julia Brace, for fund-raising: Sigourney's involvement with
Julia was, in fact, aimed at inducing the school to support the girl,
rather than to groom the girl to raise money for the school. That
said, Sigourney certainly did find in Julia Brace a natural sentimental
subject. Her poems about Brace were widely reprinted and, in all
their versions, play on the Romantic distrust of spoken language and
the idea that nonverbal ways of thinking somehow enabled one to
communicate more directly with God.

Again, when we read a work in the authentic nineteenth-century
sentimentalist tradition, it would be a mistake to assume that its play
on our emotions is an invitation to self-indulgence, as the twentieth-
century *Miracle Worker* seems to be. Nor is it, of course, an appeal
for cash. At the time these works were written, the call for empa-
thy with an abject figure in a literary work was a startling novelty,
but the poet's aim was not to shock. Rather, in presenting socially
marginal figures such as the beggar, the slave, or the deaf child as

conspecifics of middle-class readers, the purpose was to allow these readers to enter into a bond of sympathy with characters such as had not normally been possible in literary works before this time. Beggars, slaves, madmen, simpletons, and "the deaf and dumb" had previously appeared in literary works only as figures of fun or horror: the sentimentalists granted them a full measure of humanity.

The purpose of sentimentalist writers in thus championing the equal worth of every individual and the necessity of civic fairness to each was nothing less than to change the world we live in. This purpose, too, is a barrier for present-day readers, for several reasons. One is that it is difficult for us to imagine, today, a time when there was no social safety net, a time when neglect and cruelty were the expected lot of the disabled, the poor, and the enslaved, when, for example, you could actually be sold down the river or watch your newborn die from hypothermia in a house you could not afford to heat. As Andrew Delbanco has written about *Uncle Tom's Cabin*, "perhaps the fact that readers today have trouble taking seriously its heroes and villains is a tribute to its achievement—since, in some immeasurable way, it helped bring on the war that rendered unimaginable the world that Stowe attempted to imagine."[13] Sentimental literature helped to "render unimaginable" the world Sigourney lived in, and so twenty-first-century readers are rather severely handicapped in understanding her works' import. A second reason for the barrier we sense in reading sentimental works is that we have been taught to see literature in terms of aesthetics, and to be dismissive of the didactic mode, putting it into a category with propaganda and Sunday school stories. Finally, we may not be able even to recognize Sigourney's political activism, because, like all sentimental writers, she had faith in a causality that is not often acknowledged now: that a change of heart is a prerequisite to any social change.

Nineteenth-century women saw politics as of limited use. For them, families and schools, not courts and legislatures, were the agents that could change hearts and minds so that slavery, for example, would simply wither away when all Americans came to realize how wrong it was. What good, these writers might ask if they were alive today, were *Roe v. Wade* or the Americans with Disabilities Act (ADA) if most Americans decades later still retain their conservative

notions about the immorality of abortion (and of women who enjoy
sexual relations without accepting the consequences) or the worth-
lessness of people with disabilities? *Roe* became a social, legal, and
political battleground and the ADA a source of deep resentment
against disabled people seen as demanding "special treatment," because the hearts of the American citizenry had not been won to
their causes before they became laws of the land, *Roe* by Supreme
Court ruling and the ADA with bipartisan, but not popular, support.
When, in contrast, minds are changed before laws are enacted, these
laws have much better prospects, as we can see today in a cultural
battle currently playing out: gay marriage. By coming out in huge
numbers to friends and family in the last decades of the twentieth
century, gay Americans changed hearts and minds one at a time
with the result that laws discriminating against gay Americans in the
military, marriage, adoption, and so on, lagged far behind the more
progressive public sentiment. The sentimentalist writers' tack was
thus more like that of today's gay rights activists than that of disability or women's rights activists who found that their battles had
only begun when their hopes were realized in law. Sentimentalist
writers like Sigourney truly believed that not only slavery but also
drunkenness, the abrogation of Indian treaties, the neglect of deaf
children raised without language, and so on, would simply disappear
when most Americans were brought around to the belief that these
were moral wrongs. It was therefore the writer's duty to educate the
reader's heart, not agitate for premature legislation. This fundamen-
tal view of social problems, by the way, goes quite a long way toward
explaining why Sigourney never saw the need for women to vote.

In the first half of the nineteenth century, when Sigourney was
active, the works of what Hawthorne famously called the "damned
mob of scribbling women," who wrote in the sentimental tradition
and whose names are now all but forgotten, were immensely more
popular than those works we now regard as canonical. In fact, when
nonsentimentalist male authors like Hawthorne were admired, it was
for their "sympathy" and "morality," not their irony or symbolism.
But today, we are taught that the works of Hawthorne, Melville, and
Mark Twain embody universal values while the works of Sigourney,
Stowe, and other immensely popular women writers do not. In fact,
as we write in June 2011, Nobel laureate V. S. Naipaul is in the news

for saying that the works of women writers are "unequal" to his own because of their "sentimentality, the narrow view of the world" found in their work—as opposed to the universal view available to himself and other male writers, apparently. But if the actions of the crew of Melville's *Pequod* (or of Huck and Jim, or Natty Bumppo and Chingachgook—or of Hamlet and Laertes, for that matter) represent universal human themes even though more than half the readership—women and girls—are unlikely to have experienced anything remotely like such cool, arms-length male friendships, why, exactly, is the same not true of the fictive women who gather in the kitchen of Rachel Halliday, the Quaker who provides refuge for the runaway slave Eliza in *Uncle Tom's Cabin*, or of the women and girls in any of Sigourney's poems and stories about her adventures with her pupils, her former pupils, and their children? These are some of the questions we hope readers will pose themselves.

Women Writers in Antebellum New England

Women's social roles in antebellum New England were far more complex than can be summarized here, but some general statements can be made. During the first half of the nineteenth century, the United States underwent a socioeconomic shift that had at least as great an impact on women as that of what used to be disparagingly called "women's lib" in the 1960s and 1970s. In the early years of the new United States of America, homes were still the traditional production units they always had been, and the housewife was her husband's partner. By the time of the Civil War some eighty years later, the family home had become a purchasing unit, as the work most people engaged in shifted from the family's farm or cottage industry to larger-scale manufacturing and trade, taking the male breadwinner out of the home and leaving his wife and children, the only remaining members of the larger eighteenth-century household, with little to do but spend his wages. The years of Lydia Sigourney's prime of life, 1820–1840, were the very years in which married women of her class underwent a displacement from the center of household production to lives as idle ornaments kept in virtual house arrest. In a pattern almost the inverse of the transition women made in the 1970s from bored housewives to overburdened working women, women of Sigourney's generation saw their life's work taken from them, and they found themselves left not only without meaningful occupation but also without much reason or purpose for existing.

This void they filled as best they could with the idealized nuclear family. When the home had young children, it became a nursery for the new citizens of the new American Republic, who learned morality and civic virtue along with reading at their mother's knee. Any leisure time could be filled with good works like providing poor families with firewood, raising money for widows of the Greek war of independence from Turkey, or getting the men in their lives to sign a temperance pledge, in all of which enterprises Sigourney was active. Women's benevolent and moral reform societies brought lonely housewives together in such ventures, and they were regarded as extensions of women's domestic roles. Many of these societies were not charities, as we understand the word today, but rather were aimed at changing underlying social conditions, a much farther-reaching aim. Still, most middle-class women had an unprecedented amount of free time, time that the market was eager to fill by selling them commodities for which the eighteenth-century housewife had neither time nor need, such as reading materials.

Until the early nineteenth century, before the rise of the pub-lishing industry, writers could support themselves by writing only if they could find patrons for their works. Publishing houses ex-isted, but these were local enterprises that sold books, newspapers, and broadsheets in the cities in which they were located. Outside of large cities like Philadelphia, writers would not expect publica-tions to find a significant readership, let alone pay their bills, since authors were paid a flat fee for the rights to their work, no matter how well it would eventually sell. All this began to change when vast improvements in transportation allowed books and magazines to be marketed much more widely just at the time when women were finding themselves newly leisured. The "ladies'" magazines were the era's publishing phenomenon, reaching literate women over a wide geographical area and socioeconomic range, from the wives of lawyers and clergymen to minimally educated "factory girls," who were actually among their most avid readers. Relative to today's publishing scene, these magazines restricted the topics on which women could get their work published: although the magazines jumbled together widely disparate genres—poems, tales, sketches, recipes, household hints, travelogues, and pedagogical texts for the home-schooler—they did not publish any hint of cultural controversies, let alone politics. Journals with broader horizons were closed to women; until the end of the century, no work was published under a woman's name in the *North American Review*, *Knickerbocker's*, or *Atlantic Monthly*. Still, Sigourney and other women of her generation, having only the past as comparison, must have regarded the magazines as a tremendous breakthrough. Twentieth-century critics were harsh in their judgments of these periodicals, finding in them little more than "sentimental trash,"[14] but virtually all nineteenth-century women read them.

These women's magazines also made it possible for women to make careers as writers, that is, to sign their work and be paid for it, and this new outlet expanded women's ability to have their books published as well. Sigourney was a significant figure in this transition. Some historians regard her as the first American woman to support a family by her pen. She was certainly unique among women writers of the nineteenth century in having come from a working-class background rather than from the comfortable middle class of dilettante writers—and in actually needing the cash. When her husband's business concerns failed in 1837, she negotiated for book royalties of 12.5 percent and, only then, when she was the sole support of her husband, children, and stepchildren, agreed to publication under her name, "Mrs. Sigourney."

One of the most striking features of women's creative writing in the antebellum years is the appearance of women as narrative protagonists and as focal points of lyric poems. Male writers of the period rarely tried their hands at female characters (those in Hawthorne's mature works, such as Hester Prynne, the sympathetic adulteress of *The Scarlet Letter*, being prominent exceptions). In addition, conventions of the sentimental tradition—the valorization of community and relationships, the ideal of selflessness for both sexes, and the view of religious beliefs as the key to a person's power over her selfish impulses—encouraged the more careful characterization of a story's minor figures, who, in the hands of male writers, were often no more than cardboard cutouts. Women writers also gave significant roles to characters of diverse ethnicity and mixed race, in contrast to the flat characterization of the Indian, African, Pacific Islander, or mulatto in the works of Melville or Cooper, for example. Sigourney's works outside the lyric mode—her sketches, tales, and narrative poems—show carefully drawn portraits of matriarchs, Indians, and deaf children, a feature that marked women's writing as different from men's.

Despite this greater range of characterization, women writers of this period were known, and are known today, chiefly as writers of domestic scenes: "at the cradle, the hearth-stone, and the death-bed," as Sigourney herself put it.[15] In the work of some women writers, Sigourney prominent among them, domestic scenes were attempts to re-create the eighteenth-century household, the world of Sigourney's girlhood before the housewife's formerly important economic production was made obsolete, as is clear from her reference to the hearth-stone rather than the kitchen range. This nostalgia for the vanished world of the early Republic was not only a self-indulgent fantasy but should be seen, as well, as a serious attempt to re-create a social role for the middle-class women who, like Sigourney, found themselves adrift in households that had little need for the socks they could knit or the butter they could churn, such items now being readily available for purchase with Father's salary or weekly wages.

In the same essay in which she specified the cradle, hearth, and deathbed as feminine spheres of action, Sigourney also characterized feminine writing as being perfected by sorrow. Cheryl Walker is the critic most closely associated with the idea that antebellum women's literature made pain and sorrow qualifying traits of the poet, and, in line with the self-effacement that was so valued in women, this sorrow was often secret, a secret sorrow being associated with the domestic life. One could argue that Walker makes too much of this masochistic aspect of much of women's writing, but it would be a mistake to overlook it. It is well to remind ourselves of how the secret-sorrow motif would have resonated with many a nineteenth-century reader whose legal status and economic security, along with those of her children, were dependent on a drunkard, a gambler, an adulterer who brought syphilis to the marital bed, or, as in the case of Sigourney herself, a cold, selfish, failed businessman who mocked his wife about the deaths of their first three babies and badgered her into trying again, and yet again, to produce a live newborn.

Though women's writing of this period seems sometimes to wallow in self-pity, it is often forthright in its condemnation of what may be called the masculine principle. Stowe again comes to mind as the author who put men in their place—that is, on the side-lines—but Sigourney and many other writers also experimented with utopian sketches of matriarchal communities, glorifications of women's strength and ability to survive, and the inadequacy of the male psyche in the face of hardship of any sort. Judith Fetterley, in her anthology of nineteenth-century women's stories, reprints Sigourney's "The Father," calling it "a powerful fable on the primacy of the feminine principles," its critique of masculine self-importance made possible by the employment of a male narrator to achieve the appearance of "masculine self-criticism."[16] Sigourney's *Sketch of Connecticut, Forty Years Since* presents a nostalgic view not only of the traditional homestead but of the matriarch, "Madam L.," modeled on Sigourney's own patroness Jerusha Lathrop, whose benevolent rule creates a village utopia. Sigourney's oeuvre is in fact full of meditations on feminine strength as she turns the tables on the typical female sorrow by focusing on remarkable survivals rather than on victimization.

The degree to which women writers engaged in subversion to get such motifs into print becomes clear when we look at the disclaimers they typically made about their writing. Julia Ward Howe claimed to have been merely the passive transcriber of the lyrics to "The Battle Hymn of the Republic"[17] while Harriet Beecher Stowe, known in her day as the little woman who started the Civil War, disclaimed any responsibility for authorship, averring that it was God himself who wrote *Uncle Tom's Cabin*. Of course Stowe was not completely serious in this statement, but other women appear to have been genuinely horrified when their works saw print under their own names: Caroline Gilman, for example, whose poem was sent to a Boston newspaper by a friend and subsequently printed under Gilman's name, said she was "as alarmed as if I had been detected in man's apparel."[18] Women were expected to avoid the public sphere and to deprecate their own intelligence, education, and abilities. Even

Emily Dickinson ceased publication after just one go at it, while the Brontë sisters published, at first, under male pseudonyms, and Jane Austen, a shrewd manager of her publishing career, projected the artful image of herself as dear Aunt Jane, scribbling novels at a little desk in the parlor in her spare moments and caring nothing for the cash she would get for them. Jerome McGann cites a 1795 book in which a woman poet characterizes her own work as "light effusions of a youthful imagination, written at various times for the entertainment of my idle hours . . . without the knowledge of any rules; of which their irregularity is the natural consequence,"[19] and such remarks appear with some frequency from the pen of Lydia Sigourney as well, who was actually, like Austen, an astute and assiduous businesswoman.[20] It could be that this view of women as spontaneous writers was the reason that some, like Sigourney, set their stories in a historical past rather than risk a contemporary setting that might suggest to readers that any current public issues were being hinted at.

However that may be, virtually all women whose work was published portrayed themselves as Howe and Stowe did: writing spontaneously, without ambition, premeditation, or rational deliberation. The "feminine genius" was not cultivated through education, but rather "emerged naturally" through instinct alone.[21] Women were thought not to revise their work, or to have any ambition to do better. A preface to Sigourney's first book, written by Daniel Wadsworth (whom we shall meet below), announced to the world that her poems "arose from the impulse of the moment, at intervals of relaxation from such domestic employments, as the circumstance of the writer and her parents, rendered indispensable." Today, one wonders whether readers of the time were indeed reassured that the book in question did not come at the expense of an unmade bed! Sigourney, to her credit, later wrote occasional poems and statements indicating a realization that composing poetry conflicted with her duties as a housewife, and she may well have been the first woman writer to make such public statements. It is remarkable that Sigourney was able, in print, to admit to a bit of sloppy housekeeping, brushing it aside with "that's what comes from writing poetry."[22]

In spite of her subversions of the male-controlled publication venues and the patriarchal structure of home and family life, Sigourney, like most women of her generation, was not a suffragist. The Women's Rights Convention held in Seneca Falls, New York, in the summer of 1848 was convened by the cohort that had been educated by Sigourney's generation of teachers: Emma Willard, Catharine Beecher, and Sigourney herself. The radical views of Elizabeth Cady Stanton, who had been a student of Willard's, shocked and distressed her former teacher. Sigourney was perhaps more radical than Willard or Beecher in her advocacy of the right to an education not only for girls but for African American, Indian, and deaf children. Some critics, especially in the 1970s, have concluded that Sigourney's views on women's rights demonstrate that she remained "grossly ignorant of woman's plight,"[23] but that is very far from the case. We get closer to the truth if we look at how each generation builds on the one before it: Sigourney, who championed the causes of so many oppressed groups in the 1820s and 1830s, was an old woman of fifty-seven, no longer producing original work, when, in 1848, the thirty-two-year-old Cady Stanton read aloud, before a mixed audience of three hundred women and men, her declaration of the inalienable civic and social rights of women.

Alice Cogswell and the Beginnings of Deaf Education*

Before Mrs. Sigourney was a writer, she was a teacher, Miss Huntley, and it was as such that she became involved in her third liberal cause, third after education for girls and for black children (whom she had been teaching without charge on Sundays): deaf education. How, as a very young woman, she came to be involved in the founding of deaf education in the United States, how deaf children came to be subjects of her writing, and how she later disappeared from Deaf history are the subjects to which we now turn.

---

*Passages from this section appeared in another form in Sayers and Gates, "Lydia Huntley Sigourney and the Beginnings of American Deaf Education in Hartford: It Takes a Village."

Lydia Howard Huntley had been born in Norwich, Connecticut, in 1791, and was of an age with her much-better-known colleagues Thomas Hopkins Gallaudet (1787–1851) and Laurent Clerc (1785–1869), who are regarded today as the founders of deaf education in the United States. Lydia was an only child of poor parents: her father was a Revolutionary War veteran employed as a gardener for a wealthy widow, Jerusha Lathrop, mentioned above as the model for Sigourney's literary matriarch "Mrs. L." Lydia had had only a few years of formal schooling, but Mrs. Lathrop had given her access to her late husband's large library, where Lydia had educated herself and dreamed of becoming a teacher one day.

In 1805, fourteen-year-old Lydia Huntley made her first trip to Hartford, to visit Mrs. Lathrop's relatives Mrs. Jeremiah Wadsworth and her married son Daniel, who lived in adjacent mansions. As Jerusha Lathrop's protégée, Lydia was received as a member of the extended family and stayed for two weeks, entranced with the Wadsworths' collections of books and paintings and apparently not at all put off by Daniel Wadsworth's eccentricities, for which he was widely known.[24]

Just two years later, Miss Huntley, now sixteen and old enough to earn her own living, started a school in Norwich, the first of the several schools she would conduct before her marriage. The life of a village schoolteacher that she pursued for seven years could well have been her lot in life had she not received an invitation in May 1814 from the Wadsworths to visit them in Hartford for the election festivities. In those days, Hartford hosted representatives from around the state to meet on the first Thursday in May to count votes. These representatives lodged with local families for a few days, and housewives vied with one another to show the best hospitality and bake the best "election cake." She ended up staying with the Wadsworths into the summer and would have met many of their friends among their social set. It must have been during this visit in the summer of 1814 that Wadsworth offered to help Lydia see some of her poems into print: her first book, *Moral Pieces in Prose and Verse*, was brought out by a Hartford publishing house the next year and was prefaced with an essay by Wadsworth himself.

In July, Daniel Wadsworth suggested to her that, rather than return to her school in Norwich in the fall, she conduct a school in his mother's house. His purpose was "explicitly to introduce his protégée to Hartford Society,"[25] that is, to introduce her professionally, since she already would have been known as a family friend. Wadsworth decided on the number of fifteen pupils, selected them himself, and kept a waiting list. The three oldest daughters of Hartford physician Mason Fitch Cogswell, Mary, Elizabeth, and Alice, were pupils number ten, eleven, and twelve. That Alice was deaf apparently made little or no impression on Wadsworth: "As his influence in society gave him an almost unlimited choice of pupils," Sigourney wrote in her later years, "he kept in view similarity of station and of attainments" in order to make it easier to teach without "disparities that might cause jealousies and impede friendships."[26]

Alice had been deafened at age two by an illness called "spotted fever," probably meningitis, and arrived in Miss Huntley's schoolroom as a sprightly nine-year-old using what Sigourney, in the passage form *Letters of Life* reprinted here in part 1, called "animated gesture [intermingled] with a few articulate sounds . . . in a strong, guttural intonation." Miss Huntley approached the task of teaching Alice to read and write English by expanding on the visual/gestural communication Alice already employed. Years later, in a passage in *Letters to My Pupils*, also reprinted here in part 1, she would explain that because the "language of signs" and the "rapid manual alphabet" had not yet reached America, the only means of communication were "representation with both hands, of each letter constituting a word, and the few signs that we were able to invent, founded principally on visual resemblance." While this sounds fairly primitive, a story Alice signed for Miss Huntley about her charitable visit to a desperately poor family, awkwardly glossed into English by the teacher, suggests fairly competent signing for a deaf child who had no access to a community of signers. In the following passage from the same extract of *Letters to My Pupils* reprinted here, we notice, for example, the manner in which the coals and the baby are described:

> My feet were very cold. But there was not fire to warm them. No. I could have held in one small hand, those few, faint coals. Neither was there any wood. No. The poor woman lay in a low bed. Half sitting up, she shivered, for she wore only old, thin garments. And she had

a sick baby. It was pale and threw its arm about. I think it cried. But there was no doctor there. No, none.

For Alice to be signing this story after only a few months with Miss Huntley suggests that she had been signing with her family using a system more closely approaching real language than is often supposed, and that she brought her home signs to school with her.

As a lay person with regard to deaf education and "having no guide in this species of instruction," but armed with deeply held progressive pedagogical principles, as she describes herself in the same passage, Miss Huntley incorporated Alice into the school day and its lessons quite effectively. Many a mainstreamed deaf child today, languishing in a large public school with an underqualified interpreter, would envy Alice. To begin with, Miss Huntley was very well aware of Alice's intelligence, as we see in this passage, and vastly admired the girl's ability to "overleap every obstacle" of communication in order to grasp factual knowledge and come to informed conclusions. Miss Huntley, ever modest, gave all credit for Alice's success in school to the child's "originality, and considerable histrionic talent," as well as to her remarkable perseverance. To put Alice on a parallel track with her hearing classmates, though she was sorely behind them, especially in English, Sigourney describes how she arranged for her a vocabulary "of her own scholastic gleanings" by which Alice could complete a weekly review of her studies just as her classmates did at a more advanced level. Alice provided her own definitions of these words and "gave them by signs" for her classmates to interpret orally, thus giving all the pupils a stake in Alice's success.

Naturally, in the days when education was carried out by oral recitation of lessons, the deaf child was sometimes idle in the classroom, but Alice certainly was able to command the teacher's attention. Although Miss Huntley set aside regular times for one-on-one instruction, Alice was so eager that "sometimes ere the classes had quite completed their recitations, [she] stood imploringly by my side, spelling on her slender fingers, 'have you not now something for your little Alice?'" Sigourney's later sentimental effusions about her affection for Alice in *Letters to My Pupils*—"she was the darling of all"—may strike some present-day readers as patronizing, but, writing this memoir in 1856, near the end of her long life, Sigourney used the same kind of language in regard to *all* of her pupils, particularly those twenty-six of her eighty-four pupils who, like Alice, died of tuberculosis or in childbirth before reaching middle age. Sigourney calls one "a being so deservedly dear," another "ever a favorite among her school-associates," a third was "cherished" by her classmates, and all are affectionate, amiable, sweet, gentle, obedient, and loving, as, for the sentimentalist, they must be.[27]

Alice's time as a pupil in Miss Huntley's school has been denigrated by Deaf history. Harlan Lane, for example, calls Alice the school's "mascot" and describes the little girl needing virtually to beg for instruction so that she could be just like the other pupils.[28] Ample evidence, however, suggests this was far from the case. As Timothy Dwight remarked in 1866, shortly after Sigourney's death, her teaching

> was in advance of her age. She was . . . a valuable, inspiring, interesting, self-sacrificing, and loving instructor; ever considering how she might best awaken and cultivate and stimulate her pupils. . . . She seems to have studied continually the capabilities of each mind under her charge.

Dwight's last point is crucial: Miss Huntley saw each pupil as an individual whose potential was to be uniquely cultivated. The proof of her success lay in the annual reunions of pupils who, "for forty-five years . . . met together to celebrate with their honored teacher the days of their association in the school-room, and to repeat their generous testimony to the good she had bestowed upon them."[29]

And what were Thomas Hopkins Gallaudet and Laurent Clerc, the acknowledged founders of American deaf education, doing during the fall and winter of 1814–1815, the first year of Miss Huntley's school, when Alice was learning reading, writing, and arithmetic? Clerc was still teaching at the Institution Nationale des Sourds-Muets à Paris, where he had himself been educated, with no notion he would ever bring the Paris school's methods to Connecticut. Gallaudet had just graduated from Andover Seminary (though he would not be ordained until 1834) and was living with his parents next door to the Cogswells, preaching a little and traveling. It is widely taken as fact today that Gallaudet had begun to teach Alice during vacations from Andover between 1812 and 1814; the best known, but almost certainly apocryphal, tale about the two, how he taught her the word "hat," is said to have occurred on one of these visits home. This story's earliest attestation, however, is in an 1847 article by Lewis Weld, who did not know Gallaudet until 1818. Gallaudet himself claimed, more vaguely, in an 1818 *North American Review* article written by J. M. Wainwright, that he spent much of the winter of 1814–1815 teaching Alice. How that could have been accomplished is unclear: Alice was occupied in Miss Huntley's schoolroom six days a week, and Sigourney, always modest about her own achievements and ready to credit Gallaudet, fails to mention any outside tutoring at all for Alice or even any advice for herself as teacher.

It was toward the end of Alice's first year with Miss Huntley that Dr. Cogswell convened a planning session to establish a school for the deaf in Hartford. Beginning in 1812, Cogswell had been taking a census of deaf people in Connecticut (there were eighty-four) and meeting other parents interested in education for their deaf children. He knew of two American families who had sent their deaf children to a private school in Edinburgh, Scotland, the Braidwood Academy, where pupils were taught to speak. And he had corresponded with John Braidwood when the latter arrived in the United States in 1812 with the idea of founding a similar school in Philadelphia, as he had done in London. As it happened, nothing came of young Braidwood's plan. So the need was clear. The planning session that Cogswell convened in his home that April evening in 1815 brought together nine wealthy Hartford residents, including a merchant named Charles Sigourney, each of whom had already made a substantial donation to the project and who together would, that evening, determine to send a well-educated but unemployed Hartford resident, Thomas Hopkins Gallaudet, to England to study deaf education and bring the knowledge of that method back to Hartford. Gallaudet accepted the charge and departed almost immediately that May. While he was in Europe, Alice continued with Miss Huntley, developing literacy.

The earliest known letters written by Alice, dated July 6 and August 14, 1815, were both addressed to Gallaudet in England.

They were written after Alice had been in Miss Huntley's school for almost a year. An excerpt from the July 6 letter:

> I am very glad you write to me. You stay long in the ship on the waves. God loves and keeps you. I pray morning and evening, God to keep Alice and all men. He is sorry that we are wicked–I do not know so much as Mary and Elizabeth. But I am glad that I understand. I hope, I shall learn to read well before you Come back.–I love my arithmetic and my school, Miss Huntley. says. "yes you are very good, Alice."

In September of 1815, Dr. Cogswell wrote to his niece Harriet Cogswell,

> Alice improves daily. She is interesting. [illegible] at least beyond all you can conceive of. Mr. Colt told Miss Huntley a story while he was here. She told it to Alice by <u>Signs</u>. Alice immediately wrote it down for her forenoon exercise, a copy of which you have on the opposite side in her own handwriting without alterations or correctations [sic]. . . . This is the production of a child of 9 years old, who can neither hear nor speak.

Alice's composition on the back of the letter begins,

> My Dear Miss Huntley
>   I remember story, Miss Huntley was tell me. Old. many years_ Mr. colt. . little boy–Name man Peter Colt. very much curls little boy_ hair white Oh very beautiful mama lap little boy_ Comb curl love to see_ O beautiful_ one morning long man preacher_ coat black come bow ask Mama give little boy hair. . . .

Gallaudet was sent a copy of this story. Many years later, Gallaudet's son Edward Miner Gallaudet would remark that the letter "show[s] the progress she [Alice] was making under the instructions of Miss Huntley."[30] What's striking in this very early exercise in developing English literacy is not only Alice's acquisition of English vocabulary, but also what appears to be a sign-language grammar. The fragment "hair white Oh very beautiful" is easily seen as any natural sign language's HAIR WHITE as topic, then the interjection "Oh" as the translation of a sign usually glossed today as wow and used to introduce the predicate (without recourse to the copulative, here "was," which does not exist in natural signed languages), then what is said about this topic, BEAUTIFUL.* The sequence "long man preacher_ coat black come bow" looks like a sign-by-sign transcription of this sentence in today's American Sign Language (ASL), even down to the slight pause, indicated by a low dash, which signals the subject of the sentence has been given. While we can be all but certain that there was no signing community in Hartford at this date and therefore no true signed language, it does seem that the Cogswells' home sign had developed grammar typical of natural signed languages and that Sigourney was conversant with it and used it in the classroom.

Gallaudet met Laurent Clerc in May 1815 at a demonstration of deaf education in London that was given by Clerc and his colleagues Jean Massieu and the Abbé Roch-Ambroise Sicard of the Institution Nationale des Sourds-Muets à Paris, which used what they called "methodical signing" as the language of instruction. The Abbé Sicard, the principal of the school and a monarchist who had been imprisoned several times by Revolutionary forces, had fled France on Napolean's return from exile in Elba earlier that spring. Accompanying him to safety in London were his two deaf teachers, Massieu and Clerc. It was sheer luck that the three Frenchmen should have been in London during the few weeks before Napoleon's defeat at Waterloo, when they returned to Paris, at the same time that Gallaudet was investigating the Braidwood method of educating the deaf. But it wasn't until months later, February 1816 in fact, that Gallaudet resigned himself to studying the French method and left England for Paris. In the summer of 1816, he returned to the United States with Clerc, whom he had somehow convinced to leave Paris to set up a deaf school in what must have seemed to the dapper Parisian a backward and alarmingly Protestant nation. That Gallaudet was still not convinced of the legitimacy of sign or the efficacy of a sign language education is shown in an April 1816 letter he wrote to Dr. Cogswell, just before leaving France: "I have often thought how you

---

*Examples of Alice's English given by Sigourney in the excerpt from *Letters to My Pupils* in part 1 show avoidance of the copula: "Alice very afraid." "Dr. Strong dead." "Peaches and apples—sweet and good."—except in the occasional sentence that looks like something she had been taught and remembered verbatim, like "I was much shaken in the awful stage."

would wish to see me making all sorts of gestures and faces. But I am now convinced of the utility of this language of pantomime to a certain extent."[31]

The two arrived in Hartford on 22 August but left almost immediately on fund-raising tours. Until the spring of 1817, when Clerc and Gallaudet finally settled in Hartford to open the Connecticut Asylum for the Education and Instruction of Deaf and Dumb Persons, Lydia Huntley had been doing remarkably well educating Alice. Yet when the school opened, she cheerfully gave her deaf pupil up to Gallaudet and Clerc for instruction, and brought all her other pupils, and many former pupils, some of whom traveled from out of town, to the opening ceremonies.[32] Under Clerc and Gallaudet, who, after all, didn't have fourteen hearing girls to educate, Alice's written English improved markedly.

During Alice's first years at the Asylum with Gallaudet and Clerc, Miss Huntley continued her school in Mrs. Wadsworth's house but maintained an interest in the Asylum and deaf children. For example, in 1817, she arranged for a tuition waiver for two deaf sisters, Maria and Harriet Bailey from her hometown, Norwich.[33] In 1819, Lydia Huntley gave up her school to marry a member of the Asylum's board of directors, the importer, wholesaler, and banker Charles Sigourney.

Now a married woman contending with three stepchildren, serial pregnancies, and the management of a large eighteenth-century-style household that included her husband's clerks, her unmarried sister-in-law, and, eventually, her own parents, Mrs. Sigourney continued her close contact with the Asylum and its pupils. In 1821, she devised a more formal role for herself and other Hartford women of her new social class by establishing the Visiting Committee of the Asylum, a group composed of the wives of the all-male directors of the school and on which she served until her death.[34] The initial purpose of this group, as outlined in Sigourney's organization letter to her fellow "Ladies," was to provide instruction in dress and manners for the female pupils, but soon the Visiting Committee, under her direction, was arranging with the directors to support the tuition and room and board of deaf-blind Julia Brace, efforts which continued at least through 1828.[35] Sigourney's interest in Julia led to correspondence in the 1830s and 1840s with Samuel Gridley Howe of the Perkins

Institution in Boston, where, as we have seen, another deaf-blind girl, Laura Bridgman, was resident. Howe and Sigourney eventually brought the two together in Hartford, as will be told in part 2.

Sigourney kept in close contact with Alice, as well as with Alice's father and two older sisters. When she started an annual reunion of her pupils in 1822, Alice, of course, attended every year, as did Dr. Cogswell.[36] And so did the girls from the deaf school: in one year, 1826, fifty "deaf and dumb" girls, including Julia Brace, joined Sigourney's school reunion.[37] She was also close to Gallaudet and his deaf wife, the former Sophia Fowler, who had once been his pupil at the Asylum. Since the Sigourneys and the Gallaudets were near neighbors, however, there is less documentation of their friendship in the way of letters or notes sent between them. We know that Sophia Gallaudet was a member of at least one of Sigourney's women's groups, as "Mrs. Gallaudet" is marked down in 1828 for donating $5.45 worth of "goods" for Greek widows and orphans, and we can imagine Sigourney using what signing skills she had to keep this deaf matron informed at meetings.[38] (Sigourney shared her interest in the Greek war of independence from Turkey with most Romantics, including Lord Byron, who died in the cause.) Gallaudet was a fan of Sigourney's work, sending a copy of her first book of poems, the same book we saw earlier published with the help of Daniel Wadsworth in 1815, to a friend in England just before he left for Europe.[39] In her autobiography, in the passage reprinted here in part 4, Sigourney describes arguments with Gallaudet about pedagogy, with Gallaudet defending innate love of goodness as a motivating tactic and Sigourney arguing for motivating pupils with emulation and earned rewards. Most significantly, Sigourney maintained close relations with Laurent and Eliza Clerc, Eliza also having been a pupil at the Asylum. In 1836, for example, Sigourney sent a letter to Clerc thanking him for sending his daughter Sarah to play with the Sigourney children, and another wishing him and his son "bon voyage" on a trip.

Sigourney, who corresponded with poets all over the United States and England, exchanged letters with the deaf poet and reporter Laura Redden Searing (1839–1923), who published under the name "Howard Glyndon." Although none of these letters is known to have survived, young Laura Redden mentions receiving a letter from Mrs. Sigourney in 1860, and, in 1869, four years after Sigourney's death, Redden published an article about Sigourney's beloved son Andrew.[40] Clearly, the correspondence between Sigourney and Redden was quite personal, even though Sigourney was forty-eight years older.

It's not uncommon to see the work of scholars who are still largely in the dark about Sigourney's role in Deaf history interpret her genuine, historically recorded interest in deaf and deaf-blind young people as merely metaphoric—a deaf girl as metaphor for woman's voicelessness and the like.[41] What's worse are critiques that posit Sigourney's use of deaf subjects for her poems, essays, and stories as evidence of some sort of strange obsession. An example of this is Ann Douglas Wood's comment that Sigourney "actually wrote a poem celebrating a deaf marriage." "Actually"? Is, or was, a wedding of a deaf man and deaf woman an outlandish or distasteful event unlikely to happen in the real world and wholly unsuited to a commemorative poem? This same critic, by the way, refers to deaf pupils at the Asylum as "occupants of the Hartford Institute for the Blind"![42] Those remarks were published forty years ago when, perhaps, awareness of Deaf culture and history were not as great as they are today, but in a 2007 edition of selected writings by Sigourney that includes an otherwise quite professionally researched biography, we find the editor telling us that Sigourney "would also support the Asylum" on whose board of directors her husband served, as though she were following Charles's lead, and, elsewhere, that she "devoted much charitable energy and a number of poems to the disabled," by which he means the deaf. For these "facts," he gives as his sole source "disability websites."[43] In other words, although he used several archives and libraries in Hartford County to consult original documents, he seems not to have known that the American School for the Deaf and its Archives were located virtually next door and could have been likewise consulted. All such scholars and literary critics would benefit from understanding, first, that Deaf Americans have a history, and second, that Sigourney lived among and interacted with signing, deaf children and adults on a daily basis, and it would have been odd indeed had she not written about them, celebrating their marriages and mourning their deaths in verse as she did those of other friends and neighbors.

Mrs. Sigourney's Reputation in American Literary History and in Deaf History

Daniel Wadsworth died in 1848, leaving none of his fortune to the Asylum; in fact, he bequeathed a parcel of land adjacent to the school to his nephew. His positive views of deaf people, however, were unaffected by any falling out he may have had with the school. He left a plaster bust of "Mr. Laurent Clerc" and another of "Mrs. L. H. Sigourney" to the Connecticut Historical Society.[44] Did he regard these two as the founders of deaf education in America? Or one as the founder of deaf education and the other as Hartford's most famous poet? Whatever Wadsworth may have thought in 1848, the institutionalized forces of both antifeminism and professionalism were soon to bury Lydia Huntley Sigourney, even before her death seventeen years later.

When Thomas Hopkins Gallaudet died two years after Wadsworth, in 1850, the American Asylum at Hartford for the Education and Instruction of the Deaf and Dumb, as it had been called since 1819, had grown into a large and successful institution under the leadership of Lewis Weld, whom Gallaudet had hired straight out of Yale College, and who subsequently married Mary Cogswell, Alice's oldest sister. Four months after Gallaudet's death, his friends and colleagues held a memorial service for him, focused chiefly on his role in founding deaf education, although after his early retirement from the school Gallaudet had enjoyed a second career of twelve years working with "the insane." The keynote speech, "A Tribute to Gallaudet," was delivered by Henry Barnard, a Hartford native and, like Gallaudet and Weld, a Yale alumnus, who edited the *American Journal of Education* and would later serve as commissioner of education under President Grant. It is in Barnard's speech that we can see the beginnings of what Deaf historian Paddy Ladd has called the "Grand Narrative" of "distinguished hearing educators,"[45] in this case all Yale men, and the erasure of Lydia H. Sigourney from the history of deaf education.

Although Sigourney was present at Gallaudet's memorial service and was an internationally acclaimed poet, by far the most famous resident of Hartford, Barnard refers to her in these words:

the name of Lydia Huntley must not be forgotten . . . who under this and another name, by weaving her own happy inspirations into the bridal wreath and the mourning chaplet of her friends, has associated herself inseparably with the household memories of our city and our land.[46]

This "compliment" withholds Sigourney's professional nom de plume and reduces her internationally known literary oeuvre to "happy inspirations" for her friends that are now associated with Hartford households!

About Gallaudet, in contrast, this is what Barnard said:

the individual whose blessed privilege it was to plant the standard of intelligence in the almost inaccessible fastness of Alice Cogswell's mind, — to establish for her lines and avenues of communication between the inner and the outer world, — to give her the means and methods of self-culture, — and if not literally to unloose the tongue, or unseal the ear, to unfold to her spirit the harmonies, and clothe it with the singing robes of heaven, — THOMAS HOPKINS GALLAUDET.[47]

Barnard presents Alice's mind as a fortress and Gallaudet as a soldier who must storm it to plant the flag of culture. The sexual color of the metaphors used here may not have been so striking in Victorian New England as it is today, but still, it does seem remarkable to speak of the education of a little girl by a male teacher in such terms. Barnard continues,

In such methods as his own ingenuity could suggest, and what lights as he could gather from a publication of the Abbe [sic] Sicard, which Dr. Cogswell had procured from Paris, Mr. GALLAUDET from time to time succeeded in imparting to her a knowledge of many simple words and sentences which were much enlarged by members of her own family and especially by her first teacher, Miss Lydia Huntley.[48]

Thus Barnard sows the fiction, soon to be regarded as historical fact, that Gallaudet knew about French sign language education and used it to teach a previously alingual child, thus providing a model on which her family and Miss Huntley, all of whom had up until now apparently been sitting on their hands, could expand. Barnard is also quite mistaken, by the way, about the Sicard publication, a mistake that has been widely copied. There was no book by Sicard published before 1816 that would have been of any use to Cogswell or Gallaudet.

Much in the same vein are remarks by Lewis Weld. In his essay, "The American Asylum," which was published in the *American Annals of the Deaf and Dumb* and reprinted in Barnard's "Tribute," Weld relates the "hat" story and says that Gallaudet's success in teaching Alice

> led to a very intimate intercourse with the child and her father's family during intervals of relaxation from professional studies through several years, and resulted in her acquiring so much knowledge of simple words and sentences as satisfied her friends that she might learn to write and read, and that Mr. Gallaudet of all in the circle of their acquaintance, was the person best qualified to undertake her instruction.[49]

Weld, like Barnard—and like Gallaudet himself—seems to be expanding the dates and the extent to which Gallaudet engaged in teaching English words to Alice.

In 1859, the Rev. Heman Humphrey, a friend from Yale College, compiled Gallaudet's letters, speeches, and sermons into a narrative biography, in which he says that Gallaudet "succeeded, better than anyone else, in conversing with [Alice] by manual signs, and teaching her the names of persons and things by simple sentences." After naming all of Gallaudet's outstanding qualifications, Humphrey goes on to claim that Gallaudet was "preeminently qualified for the task of pouring light of a new being into [deaf children's] dark minds" and was "the first pioneer in this difficult system of education."[50]

Weld, Humphrey, Barnard, Gallaudet himself: all Yale men, all relating the same story of Alice's alleged abysmal ignorance when Gallaudet first encountered her, and of Gallaudet's talent, dedication, piety, and success.

Mrs. Sigourney died in 1865, at age seventy-four. Deaf Hartford had not forgotten her: the entire student body of the Asylum appeared at her funeral.[51] But a steady flow of Yale men into teaching positions at the Hartford school ensured that the official record of deaf education in Hartford would be both inclined and well situated to denigrate Sigourney's contributions—every principal until well into the twentieth century, and the first *nineteen* hearing teachers, in a school that had only a handful of teachers at any one time and that tended to keep nearly all of them until retirement, all came straight from Yale.[52] The following year, 1866, on the publication of her posthumous autobiography, *Letters of Life*, Sigourney was mocked by the Yale establishment in a review published in *The New Englander* (later the *Yale Review*) by one of its editors, Timothy Dwight (who would later serve as president of Yale from 1886–1899). Dwight claimed Sigourney was a running joke in Hartford, accused her of vanity and self-aggrandizement, ridiculed her literary style, and wondered whether she stayed in love with her husband after marriage![53] In reality, Dwight and many other readers must have been shocked by the very fact of a woman having written an autobiography, implying thereby that she was the center of her own story,[54] and he was unlikely to be aware of the esteem in which literary women of his day held Sigourney, because, of course, their reviews and critiques were not publishable in the all-male Ivy League magazines that Dwight read, and wrote for. Unfortunately, while the comments of Dwight's female contemporaries were forgotten, his derisive review was widely parroted, for example in a 1922 sketch of Mrs. Sigourney and in the only biography written of her—by Yale professor Gordon Haight, published in 1930 by Yale. Even Harlan Lane's seminal history of the founding of the deaf school in Hartford puts Dwight's derision into the mouth of his narrator, a fictionalized Clerc![55]

In 1886, the monumental *Memorial History of Hartford County, Connecticut* was brought out, establishing the facts about Sigourney and the Asylum as they were then interpreted, at the height of the Victorian Age, and as they would be received in the twentieth century. Sigourney is covered in a section called "Hartford in Literature," and though she was by far the best published author in the history of the city, she is given just one paragraph in the nineteen-page article, the conclusion of which is that she "enjoyed in her day a vogue which the present generation finds . . . hard to account for."[56] The author, Henry Beers, was professor of English at Yale College, which did not admit women to its undergraduate program until 1969, so it is easy to understand why someone in his position might give short shrift to a "poetess" whose formal schooling ceased at age thirteen. However, Professor Beers was also the grandson of Laurent and Eliza Clerc. For Beers to have written such a scathing paragraph about one of his grandfather's first friends in America and the woman who did so much for the school his grandmother attended suggests a conscious, if unacknowledged, effort to consolidate the male-centric, Yale-centric Grand Narrative of deaf education.

In this same monumental *Memorial History*, the entry on the American Asylum was written by someone who had the best of reasons for upholding the Grand Narrative and portraying Thomas Hopkins Gallaudet as the savior to the deaf: his youngest son, Edward Miner Gallaudet. E. M. Gallaudet's entry on the school makes no mention whatsoever of Alice Cogswell's having had an earlier teacher or of the fact that she was already functionally literate when the Asylum opened its doors in 1817. Nine years after this article appeared, E. M. Gallaudet, who was in fact a college dropout, received an honorary doctoral degree—from Yale.

Just two years after the publication of the *Memorial History*, E. M. Gallaudet's 1888 *Life of Thomas Hopkins Gallaudet* added further spin to the Grand Narrative by claiming that Gallaudet "induced [Alice's] parents to place her under the direct instruction of Miss Huntley."[57] Of course Gallaudet could not have done any such thing since the invitation of pupils was, as we have seen, entirely at the discretion of Daniel Wadsworth. By 1891, the Deaf community was being told by one of its own newspapers, *The Silent Worker*, that "for two or three years [Sigourney] was a teacher of the deaf *under the elder Gallaudet*."[58]

Sigourney continued to be treated with "almost universal contempt"[59] until the late twentieth century, when scholars such as Nina Baym, Jane L. Donawerth, Mark David Hall, Mary Hershberger, Sarah Robbins, Melissa Ladd Teed, Emily S. Watts, and Sandra A. Zagarell, to name but a few, began to recognize the true importance of her literary work and social activism. Watts, in her study *The Poetry of American Women*, points out that Sigourney's remarkable ability to place her work so widely gave her the means to reach a huge readership throughout the United States and Great Britain and thereby to educate the public about their social and moral responsibilities toward the have-nots of America and the world. Scholars today realize that Sigourney, like Hannah More in England, worked all her life to promote women's rhetorical spaces in "teaching, conversation, reading aloud, . . . and letter-writing" *because* they were denied a voice in public discourse.[60]

Emily Watts points to Sigourney's 1834 *Poems* as representing her best work. Interestingly, that particular volume includes a great many poems on or mentioning deaf people—"Marriage of the Deaf and Dumb," "Meeting of the Blind with the Deaf, Dumb, and Blind," "On Seeing the Deaf, Dumb, and Blind Girl Sitting for her Portrait," and "Alice." Throughout her career as a writer, Sigourney wrote about people she knew and held them up as inspiration for her reading public.

In 1924, Grace Cogswell Root said that we will never "know the relative importance of the parts played by [Alice's] two teachers Miss Huntley and the Reverend Gallaudet in bringing her into our world of speech and hearing. It would be interesting to say definitely how this exciting game was played."[61] We may never know for sure, but there is no doubt that Lydia H. Sigourney's contribution to the early education of Alice Cogswell was a vital element in the founding of deaf education in America, and that her subsequent publications on the Asylum and deaf people greatly enabled the wide acceptance throughout the country of public education for deaf children.

Lydia Sigourney was a woman of her time, conventional in many ways, but a trendsetter and quite the original personality. Of the women writers of her generation, Sigourney alone was not born into the middle class, but she became the mouthpiece of middle-class domesticity. She aimed to be an "instrument of good" and carried on an "obvious public program" of promoting oppressed groups, yet she came to be regarded as a sentimental hack and a housewife who knitted stockings as she composed vapid poems to order so as not to lose time from domestic responsibilities.[62] Her poems "reflect the culmination of the sentimental cult of motherhood," but she suffered the deaths of all but one of her children and, apparently, the scorn of both her stepdaughters, one of whom is said to have "danced around the room in mockery when Lydia Sigourney's mother died."[63] Her own son, in fact, was "ashamed of her success as a writer," and her husband claimed that he could not value a wife who, by signing her work, was "the public property of the whole community,"[64] a sentiment, by the way, that Charles Sigourney shared with Samuel Gridley Howe, whose wife dared to sign her own name to the lyrics for "The Battle Hymn of the Republic." Instead of dramatically dying in her youth like Byron and Shelley, Sigourney, like Wordsworth, lived more than long enough to lose any originality and become predictable, in fact, repetitive. She "was a major event in the history of women and literature in nineteenth-century America,"[65] but she was mocked by the Yale literary establishment in her lifetime and became the object of the contempt and hostility of some twentieth-century critics, including feminists who might have been expected to know better. Quite apart from subjective appreciations, it is indisputable that she pioneered bilingual English/natural-sign education for a mixed classroom of deaf and hearing pupils at a time when even the French "methodical sign" approach was as yet unknown here. At her death at age seventy-four, more than two dozen schools were educating deaf children in this country, and the future Gallaudet University, which continues to provide post-secondary education to deaf people in ASL to this day, was already granting its first degrees.

Timeline

Events in Lydia Huntley Sigourney's life and events in Deaf history appear in roman type; other historical events appear in italic type. Sigourney's poems and prose pieces reprinted in this volume are in bold.

1785   Laurent Clerc is born in La Balme, Canton of Cremieu, Department of Isère, France.

1787   Thomas Hopkins Gallaudet is born in Philadelphia.

The Constitutional Convention meets and drafts the U.S. Constitution, leaving slavery intact.

1789   *George Washington becomes the first president of the new United States of America.*

The French Revolution commences.

Charles-Michel de l'Épée, founder and director of the Institution Nationale des Sourds-Muets à Paris, dies in December. His successor is Roch-Ambroise Sicard, a royalist, who will be in prison or in exile for much of the Revolution.

1790   *Benjamin Franklin dies at age eighty-four, shortly after throwing his weight behind a petition to Congress from the Pennsylvania Abolition Society to abolish slavery in the new nation.*

1791   Lydia Howard Huntley is born in Norwich, Connecticut.

1794   *Red Jacket and other Iroquois leaders sign the Treaty of Canandaigua, giving up much of their land in exchange for peace with the United States, after having fought on the side of the British during the Revolutionary War.*

1797   Clerc goes to Paris to enter school at the Institution
Nationale des Sourds-Muets, under the interim director,
deaf teacher Jean Massieu.

1798   *William Wordsworth and Samuel Coleridge*, Lyrical Ballads

1804   Napoleon proclaimed emperor.

1805   Alice Cogswell is born in Hartford.

Clerc finishes his education and is given a trial appointment
as a tutor.

Gallaudet graduates from Yale and returns to his parents'
home in Hartford.

Fourteen-year-old Lydia Huntley makes her first visit to
the Wadsworths in Hartford.

*Red Jacket addresses the U.S. Senate to defend Native American
religious beliefs against Christian evangelism with his speech
"Religion for the White Man and the Red."*

1806   Clerc is appointed teacher and takes over the highest class.

1807   Alice Cogswell becomes deaf.

Lydia Huntley opens her first school in Norwich.

Gallaudet returns to Yale for a master's degree and will
remain as a tutor.

1810   Gallaudet leaves his tutoring position at Yale and becomes
a traveling salesman.

1812   Dr. Cogswell begins to investigate deaf education.

U.S. declares war on Great Britain.

Gallaudet enrolls at Andover Seminary.

1814 Twenty-three-year-old Lydia Huntley is invited to visit the Wadsworths again; Daniel Wadsworth offers to establish a school for her. The school opens in the fall with fifteen pupils. Alice Cogswell is among them.

Gallaudet graduates from Andover at age twenty-seven and is licensed to preach, but is not ordained. He declines three calls to the ministry and lives with his parents.

The Treaty of Ghent ends War of 1812.

Napoleon is exiled to Elba.

Sicard returns to Paris.

1815 Lydia Huntley's *Moral Pieces in Prose and Verse*, including "**For Alice**," "**Excuse for not Fulfilling an Engagement**," and a preface by Daniel Wadsworth.

March *Napoleon returns to Paris from Elba.*

April Dr. Cogswell convenes a planning meeting to establish a school for the deaf in Hartford.

Gallaudet is asked to travel to Europe to study educational methods.

May Sicard flees to London, taking Laurent Clerc and Jean Massieu with him.

Gallaudet embarks for London.

June Gallaudet meets Sicard, Massieu, and Clerc in London.

Napoleon defeated at Waterloo.

Sicard, Clerc, and Massieu return to Paris.

July, August Alice writes her first known letters; these are to Gallaudet, whom she knows to be researching deaf education abroad.

1816 Spring Gallaudet leaves London for Paris; he takes private lessons in sign language from Clerc.

August Gallaudet returns to the United States with Clerc; Clerc and Alice meet on August 22.

American Colonization Society (ACS) founded to settle emigrant slaves in Africa.

1817 Connecticut Asylum at Hartford for the Instruction of Deaf and Dumb Persons opens on April 15 with seven pupils: Alice transfers from Miss Huntley's school.

Lydia Huntley arranges for a tuition waiver at the Asylum for Maria and Harriet Bailey of Norwich.

Lewis Weld is recruited by Gallaudet to teach at the Asylum.

1818 *The disestablishment of the Congregational Church in Connecticut.*

New York School for the Deaf is founded.

The *North American Review*, the nation's first and foremost literary magazine, publishes a long letter from J. M. Wainwright about the American Asylum in Hartford. This letter includes a statement by Gallaudet, writing of himself in the third person and characterizing himself as Alice Cogswell's teacher, without mentioning that she was in school elsewhere.

Mary Shelley, Frankenstein, Or, The Modern Prometheus.

1819 Clerc marries his former pupil Eliza Crocker Boardman of Troy, New York. Lewis Weld is a groomsman.

Lydia Huntley marries Charles Sigourney.

Henry Clay is instrumental in securing federal funding for the Asylum.

The first two cantos of Lord Byron's Don Juan *are published anonymously; they create a scandal.*

1820   The Pennsylvania School for the Deaf is founded.

Sigourney gives birth to a stillborn daughter.

The Missouri Compromise, engineered by Henry Clay, averts the first crisis concerning the extension of southern slavery to the western frontier.

1821   Sigourney gives premature birth to a son, who dies.

Sigourney creates the Ladies' Visiting Committee of the Asylum.

Gallaudet marries a former Asylum pupil, Sophia Fowler.

The Asylum moves to new location at 690 Asylum Hill, a property purchased with a federal grant arranged by Henry Clay.

Emma Willard opens the Troy Female Seminary, the first institution offering postsecondary education to women in the United States.

The Greek war of independence from Turkey begins.

1822   Sigourney begins efforts to enroll sixteen-year-old Julia Brace at the Asylum by campaigning for tuition support.

Sigourney, *Traits of the Aborigines of America.*

1823   Alice completes her seven-year course of study at the Asylum and leaves school at age eighteen.

The Kentucky School for the Deaf is founded.

James Fenimore Cooper, The Pioneers.

Sigourney gives birth to a second premature son, who also dies.

1824   "A Young Lady of 27 Years of Age" writes an essay on her ideas of the sun, moon, etc., before her education at the Asylum; it is published in the Asylum's Annual Report.

Sigourney, *Sketch of Connecticut, Forty Years Since.*

Lord Byron dies while fighting for Greece in its war for independence, leaving his masterpiece, Don Juan, *unfinished.*

Samuel Gridley Howe graduates from Harvard Medical School and joins the Greek army at age twenty-three.

The Hartford Retreat for the Insane opens its doors.

1825 Julia Brace is enrolled at the American Asylum at age eighteen.

Sigourney dines with President John Quincy Adams in the White House; meets Thomas Jefferson at Monticello and James Madison at Montpelier.

1826 "To Alice."

The American Temperance Society is founded in Boston

1827 **"Les Sourds Muets se trouvent-ils malheureux?"** **"Opinions of the Uneducated Deaf and Dumb,"** and **"On Seeing the Deaf, Dumb, and Blind Girl of the American Asylum, Hartford, at a Festival."**

Phebe and Frances Hammond are enrolled at the Asylum.

Sigourney asks her husband for a formal separation; he refuses, warning her against the appearance of feminism.

Samuel Gridley Howe returns to America to raise money for the Greek war of independence.

1828 Untitled poem beginning **"You ask 'how music melts away'**; **"The Deaf, Dumb, and Blind Girl"**; and **"Prayers of the Deaf and Dumb."**

Sigourney gives birth to a daughter, Mary, who will survive her.

Andrew Jackson is elected president.

Sophia Fowler Gallaudet donates $5.45 to Sigourney's charity for Greek widows and orphans.

1829 In the last letter she wrote before her death, Phebe Hammond describes Red Jacket's visit to the Asylum.

The Perkins School, the first school for the blind in the United States, is founded in Boston by Samuel Gridley Howe.

The Ohio School for the Deaf is founded.

1830 Dr. Cogswell dies.

Alice Cogswell dies.

Sigourney gives birth to a son, Andrew, who will die of tuberculosis as a young man.

Gallaudet resigns from the Asylum; Lewis Weld becomes principal.

Gallaudet, *The Child's Book on the Soul.*

After a coeducational secondary schooling, Elizabeth Cady is denied admission to Union College in Schenectady because of her sex; she enrolls in the Troy Female Seminary under Emma Willard.

President Andrew Jackson signs the Indian Removal Act.

The July Revolution in France overthrows Charles X; Samuel Gridley Howe is present in Paris and fights with the rebels.

1831 "Alice."

1832 *Greek independence is recognized.*

1833 ***Memoir of Phebe P. Hammond: A Pupil in the American Asylum at Hartford.***

The American Anti-Slavery Society is founded by William Lloyd Garrison and Arthur Tappan. Founding members include Frederick Douglass, Lewis Weld's brother Theodore Dwight Weld, and John Greenleaf Whittier, whose poems would be anthologized with Sigourney's later in the century.

1834 **"Marriage of the Deaf and Dumb," "On Seeing the Deaf, Dumb, and Blind Girl, Sitting for Her Portrait," "Meeting of the Blind with the Deaf, Dumb, and Blind," and "A Little Girl to her Friend."**

Gallaudet is ordained.

Samuel Gridley Howe visits the Asylum at Hartford to meet Julia Brace.

1835 **"Funeral of Dr. Mason F. Coggswell"; "The Mute Boy."**

1836 *Ralph Waldo Emerson*, Nature.

Charles Sigourney loses his bank position; his wholesale hardware business then fails.

1837 Gallaudet becomes the volunteer chaplain at the Hartford county jail.

Laura Bridgman is enrolled at the Perkins Institution for the Blind.

1838 **"Laura Bridgman, the Deaf, Dumb, and Blind Girl, at the Institution for the Blind in Boston."**

Charles Dickens, Oliver Twist.

Gallaudet becomes chaplain at the Hartford Retreat for the Insane.

The Trail of Tears results from the Indian Removal Act.

1839 During the Amistad case, the New York Institution for the Deaf and Dumb provides both picture books and a former teacher, George E. Day (Yale 1833), to communicate with, and teach, the imprisoned Africans from the ship.

Edgar Allan Poe, "The Murders in the Rue Morgue."

The Virginia School for the Deaf and the Blind is founded.

1840   *Elizabeth Cady Stanton is denied participation in the International Anti-Slavery Convention in London because of her sex; she meets the Quaker abolitionist Lucretia Mott.*

1841   Laura Bridgman meets Julia Brace.

The deaf British writer "Charlotte Elizabeth" completes her autobiography, *Personal Recollections*, which includes extensive narrative about a signing deaf child she tutored.

1842   Charles Dickens visits the United States, where he meets Laura Bridgman. His account of his trip, *American Notes*, published later this year, will be read more than forty years later by Kate Keller and inspire her to seek advice on educating her daughter Helen.

1843   The Indiana School for the Deaf is founded by William Willard, an alumnus of the American Asylum in Hartford.

1845   **Scenes in My Native Land.**

The Tennessee School for the Deaf is founded.

The North Carolina School for the Deaf is founded.

1846   The Illinois School for the Deaf is founded.

The Georgia School for the Deaf is founded.

Sigourney, "Legend of Pennsylvania."

Samuel Gridley Howe and Julia Ward Howe become active in the abolition movement.

1847   *American Annals of the Deaf and Dumb* (later, *American Annals of the Deaf*) begins publication. It is typeset and printed by pupils at the North Carolina School for the Deaf.

Laurent and Eliza Boardman Clerc's grandson Henry A. Beers is born.

1848 **"La Petite Sourde-Muette."**

Elizabeth Cady Stanton and Lucretia Mott organize the Women's Rights Convention in Seneca Falls, New York.

Samuel Gridley Howe founds the Massachusetts School for Idiotic Children.

1849 The South Carolina School for the Deaf is founded.

1850 *The U.S. Congress passes the Fugitive Slave Act.*

Nathaniel Hawthorne, The Scarlet Letter.

The Arkansas School for the Deaf is founded.

Sigourney's son, Andrew, dies of tuberculosis.

1851 Gallaudet dies of dysentery at age sixty-four.

"Hymn."

The Missouri School for the Deaf is founded.

Herman Melville, Moby-Dick.

1852 *Harriet Beecher Stowe,* Uncle Tom's Cabin.

Elizabeth Cady Stanton and Susan B. Anthony join the temperance movement.

The Wisconsin School for the Deaf is founded.

The Louisiana State School for the Deaf is founded.

1854 *Henry David Thoreau,* Walden.

The Michigan School for the Deaf is founded.

The Mississippi School for the Deaf is founded.

1855 ***Sayings of the Little Ones.***

Samuel Wadsworth Longfellow, Hiawatha.

Walt Whitman, Leaves of Grass.

The Iowa School for the Deaf is founded.

1856 *Letters to My Pupils.*

1857 The Texas School for the Deaf is founded.

1858 *American Annals of the Deaf and Dumb* publishes a debate concerning the formation of a deaf state in the West.

The Alabama School for the Deaf is founded.

Abraham Lincoln, Republican candidate for the Illinois Senate, and the incumbent senator Stephen Douglas, hold a series of seven debates on the issue of slavery.

1859 American daguerreotypist Augustus Washington writes a friendly letter to Sigourney from Liberia.

1860 *Lincoln elected president; South Carolina secedes from the Union.*

Laura Redden, a deaf woman soon to make her name as a battlefield reporter on the Civil War and, later, as a poet, receives a letter from Sigourney.

Julia Brace leaves the Asylum, at age fifty-three, to live with a sister.

1861 *Confederate troops fire on Fort Sumter, launching the Civil War.*

Pupils at the North Carolina School for the Deaf print paper currency for the Confederacy.

1864 Lincoln signs the authorization for the Columbia Institution for the Instruction of the Deaf and Dumb and the Blind in Washington, D.C., to award college degrees. This institution will later be called Gallaudet College, now University.

John Greenleaf Whittier, "Barbara Frietchie."

1865 Sigourney dies at age seventy-four.

Charles Dickens, "Doctor Marigold," a story about a deaf child who attends a sign language school and marries a classmate.

The Thirteenth Amendment outlaws slavery.

Lincoln is assassinated.

1866   *Letters of Life.*

1867   The Clarke School, the first permanent oral school for the deaf in the United States, is founded in Northampton, Massachusetts.

1869   Clerc dies at the age of eighty-four.

North Carolina opens the first separate school in the nation for black deaf children.

1870   *The Fifteenth Amendment gives African American men the right to vote.*

1874   *Edward Alexander Bouchet is the first African American to receive a bachelor's degree from Yale.*

1881   Gallaudet College admits women.

1920   *The Nineteenth Amendment gives women the right to vote.*

1950   Gallaudet College admits its first known African-American student, Andrew Foster. He goes on to graduate in 1954.

1969   *The first human sets foot on the moon.*

Yale admits women as undergraduates.

About the Texts

All of Sigourney's poems that were published more than once were altered, if only very slightly, at nearly each new appearance. Except in the case of "On Seeing the Deaf, Dumb, and Blind Girl of the American Asylum, Hartford, at a Festival," for which alternate opening stanzas are given, no attempt has been made to show such variation.

We have retained Sigourney's spelling and punctuation in all cases except those few in which a typographical error is obvious, as when the word is spelled correctly elsewhere in the same essay, story, or poem. Such printing errors have been silently corrected. This means that when Sigourney spells "Cogswell" as "Coggswell" and leaves it in that spelling over several editions of her collection *Zinzendorff, and Other Poems*, that is the way we present it.

Spelling in antebellum America did not yet uniformly conform to the innovations proposed by West Hartford native Noah Webster and codified in his dictionaries, so Sigourney's works have a bit of a British look, with spellings like "centre," "chequer," "recognise," and "Saviour." We also find words like *instructor* and *visitor* sometimes spelled with *-er*. Double *l*s are found reduced to single, and vice versa, so we find "untill" and "instil." Sigourney habitually indicates whether preterit-tense verbs ending in *-ed* are to be pronounced with or without the additional syllable: an apostrophe in place of the *e* as in "gaz'd" and "moan'd" indicates pronunciations with no additional syllable for the suffix, while the *-ed* spelling usually means that the suffix is to be pronounced as a separate syllable as in "saluted"—or "fixed," which must be pronounced "fix-ed" to fit the meter of the poem. This convention is like that seen in more familiar shortened pronunciations of *over* as "o'er" or *never* as "ne'er."

Words that are common today but that had slightly different meanings in Sigourney's time are glossed to the right of the line in which they appear, or, in prose, at the bottom of the page. Four such words used very frequently, however, are not glossed at each appearance: *peculiar, friends, cell,* and *train.* The word *peculiar* never means "odd" and always means "unique to the person": "peculiar to themselves," "her peculiar misfortune," "peculiarly affecting." The word *friends* commonly denoted, at this date, family or relatives, not people one otherwise feels close to. The word *cell* never refers to rooms in prisons or monasteries, but, for Sigourney, means any private room such as in a dormitory or hospital and sometimes means any private abode at all, such as the Cogswell family home in "Funeral of Mason F. Coggswell" or even an igloo in "Laura Bridgman." We also see *cell* used metaphorically in "La Petite Sourde-Muette" and "Meeting of the Blind with the Deaf, Dumb, and Blind," where the deaf girls' minds reside in a "guarded cell" or "hermit-cell." The word *train* denotes, at this date, only a group of people and is used by Sigourney to mean not a retinue or suite of followers, but more generally any group of people who come or go as a group, so that "yon mute train" means "that group of deaf people over there" while "the white rob'd train of peace" refers to the angels in heaven.

Finally, the expression "deaf and dumb" was the standard, unimpeachable, and, indeed, only current denominator for people we now call "deaf" or "Deaf." Alice Cogswell, in her correspondence, uses the charming abbreviation "D & D" to refer to herself, her classmates, and Mr. Clerc.

Part 1

Alice

Alice Cogswell (1805–1830) was naturally the subject, the addressee, or the impetus for many of Sigourney's poems about deaf people. Her early childhood and seven years as a student at the Asylum are relatively well documented, but we know nothing about her life between the time she completed her studies under Clerc and Gallaudet and her early death, just as we know nothing of her mother's life. Sigourney wrote only of Alice's childhood, perhaps out of personal nostalgia for those happy years as a teacher before her marriage, as well as sentimentalist avoidance of educated, middle-class adults as subjects. Alice's portrait was never painted, although a childhood silhouette was made and has survived. Even the obituary poem (in this section) that Sigourney wrote on her seems to place her back into her childhood family. Why she did not marry, as so many of her classmates did, or what she did with her time in her parents' home, whether needlework or charitable pursuits, are complete mysteries, never mentioned in the historical record. Perhaps she was already suffering the early stages of tuberculosis when she completed her course of study at the Asylum.

"For Alice" (1815)

This poem was composed when Sigourney was twenty-four-year-old Miss Lydia Huntley, during her first year of teaching Alice and fourteen other Hartford girls in Mrs. Wadsworth's house. It is not clear whether Sigourney first met Alice in her new schoolroom in the fall of 1814 or whether the first meeting had occurred earlier that year, or even on one of her earlier trips to Hartford. In any case, this seems to be Sigourney's first effort to write about Alice.

"For Alice" includes two conventional conceits about deaf people. One, expressed in stanza 3, is the notion common among all types of Romantics that the deaf person is protected against the possibility that "mad folly" might take control of her thoughts and actions, and she is therefore, "perchance," in possession of a purer soul, a soul that more closely reflects the conditions of heaven. The other conventional conceit, expressed in stanza 5, is that the deaf person will speak and hear in the afterlife, and that her voice will be all the "brighter" and her enjoyment of the "harmony of Heaven" all the greater by virtue of her having been deaf in life. Notice, though, that in true sentimentalist fashion, what the deaf hear in heaven is music and the sound of a loved one's voice—they do not communicate in speech per se because spoken language is an aspect of our fallen world and is not needed when one is free of this earthly existence.

The first two stanzas, in contrast, present fresh ideas deriving from observation of the little deaf girl: the expressive power of her "glance," and her ability by means of facial expression to form affectional bonds with the poet, that is, to excite and reciprocate feelings of "tenderness." At this point in her relationship with Alice, Sigourney most likely did not have much ability to communicate with the little girl in her home signs.

"For Alice" seems never to have been published, or titled—"For Alice" is the inscription that precedes the poem in the manuscript. This text is from a handwritten and undated "copy of Manuscript poem by Miss Huntley, 1815. Loaned by Col. Norton" in the Gallaudet Archives, Balfour MSS160, Box 15, Folder 9.

For Alice

Hartford, Tuesday, March 6th, 1815

1.

Dear little girl:—whose brow portrays
The fairest seal by Nature set;
Whose quick, expressive glance displays
The bosom's rapture or regret,—

2.

What though thy sealed lip must still
No thought of tenderness convey,
Well canst thou wake its warmest thrill
And well that warmest thrill repay.

3.

Preserved from folly's mad control
Perchance more pure to you is given
The secret utterance of the soul
Which incense best perpetuates heaven.

4.

And if at last thy gentle mind
Whe[n] shades of mortal difference cease
Still more exalted, more refined
Shall join the white rob'd train of peace.

5.

Then to what sweet seraphic voice
Shall brighter tone of praise be given
And Oh what ear shall more rejoice
To drink the harmony of Heaven.

"To Alice" (1826)

Like the 1815 "For Alice," "To Alice" was never published or titled,
the phrase "To Alice" being the opening inscription. The only
known copy is in Alice's autograph album, held by the Archives of
the American School for the Deaf, West Hartford. This "Album"
also contains a second hitherto unpublished poem by Sigourney, the
untitled poem reprinted later in this section and beginning "You ask
'how music melts away.'" "To Alice" is written out on both sides
of a leaf that has crumbled at its bottom edges and has allowed the
ink on each side to bleed through, making it difficult and, in some
passages, impossible to read. Sigourney used most of the lines of
stanzas 1–3 in a poem she published the following year, "Opinions

of the Uneducated Deaf and Dumb" (in part 2), whose subject is an unidentified pupil of the Asylum. Using this published poem to fill in illegible lines in stanza 3 leaves us with only two lacunae in stanza 4.

Alice Cogswell was twenty-one, had finished her schooling, and was living at home with her parents when Sigourney composed this poem, yet the focus is on the remembered little girl just past her tenth birthday that Alice was when she became Sigourney's pupil. According to this poem (and many other accounts), she was a happy child, though ignorant of Christian beliefs, and Sigourney begins by trying to account for that contradiction: Alice has the natural "bliss" of childhood and the "innocent sensibility" that causes her family to love her, so she is happy as long as she does not consider the "eternal question, fathomless and dread" of who made the transient world, a world that, to a deaf child, must be a nightmarish "maze"—or so Sigourney imagines it. Since these lines are also employed to describe the unnamed child of "Opinions," it is not certain which child Sigourney had in mind.

Sigourney takes up Alice's sign-language education in the third stanza, which, being the most damaged section of the poem, is heavily restored from "Opinions." The "hands that burst the chain" would apparently have been Gallaudet's. Here we have the conventional conceit, which Sigourney will use again, most poignantly in "Prayers of the Deaf and Dumb," that God understands the deaf child's prayers, though other people cannot.

The final stanza, which does not appear in "Opinions," provides another instance in Sigourney's work of the notion that deaf people become hearing in heaven. Here, she imagines the bliss Alice will feel when the first thing she will hear, after death, is praises for Jesus' love sung to the accompaniment of harps.

To Alice

[1]

Sweet friend, with silent lips—The world to thee
Was first a maze and all things moving on
In darkness and mystery. And *He*

Who made these beauteous things which fade anon
What was He? From thy brow the roses fled,
At that eternal question, fathomless and dread.

[2]

True, childhood's bliss was in thine eye,
And o'er thy features gay would rove
    That innocent sensibility
        Which wakens love
    A mother's fond caress
    A sister's tenderness
Bade through the breast the tides of pleasure run,
    A father's smile would bless
        His dear and voiceless one,
    Yet sometimes bending o'er thy sleeping bed
Their mingled tears for thee in sympathy were shed.

[3]

Oh! snatched from ignorance and pain
    And taught with seraph eye
At yon unmeasured orbs to gaze
And trace amid their quenchless blaze
    Thy own high destiny.
Forever bless the hands that burst thy chain
[And] led thy gentle steps to Learning's hallow'd fane*   *temple
    Though from thy guarded portal press
    No word of tuneful tenderness,
    In the starting tear, the glowing cheek
    The *soul* with emphasis doth speak,
        Her tone is in the sigh
        Her language in the eye,
    Her voice of harmony, a life of praise,
Best understood by *Him*,—who notes our secret ways.

[4]

The tomb shall burst these fetters—Death sublime
    Shall bear away the ills which life entail'd,
Eternity shall rend that seal which Time
    So long bewail'd.

Thou who no melody of earth hast known
Nor chirp of birds, their wind-rock'd cells that rear,
   Nor waters murmuring lone
   The organ's solemn peal, nor viol clear
Nor warbling breath of man that joins the hymning [tone?]
   Can speech of mortals tell
   What tides of bliss shall swell
If the *first* summons to they waken'd ear
Should be the plaudit of thy Savior's love,
   The golden harps that through the immortal g[rove?]
Breathe the enraptur'd strains of the redeem'd.

                              Lydia Sigourney
[Hartfo]rd, Thursday, August 4, 1826

Excerpt on Alice from *Letters of Life* (1866), including "Les Sourds Muets se trouvent-ils malheureux?" (1827)

When Sigourney's autobiography appeared in 1866, a year after her death, it would have surprised the reading public that a woman would even think of writing the story of her life. Sigourney was likely trying to soften this response by framing the book as a series of letters to a "dear friend" who has asked for an account of her life. The deaf Englishwoman who wrote as "Charlotte Elizabeth" and who, like Sigourney, was a teacher, and was very religious and estranged from her husband, likewise chose the letter form for her memoirs in 1841.

Sigourney's tone in the book is nostalgic, as she lovingly re-creates her years as a girl at home and as a young woman starting out on life—she doesn't marry until page 261 of the 400-page book, and virtually nothing is said of Charles Sigourney after the wedding. And no wonder: after suffering a stillbirth, two infant deaths, and eight years of what seems to have been continuous badgering about her duty to him every time she visited her parents, she had asked him for a formal separation in 1827, which he refused to grant. The chapter from which this excerpt is taken, "Educational Reminiscences," details her childhood ambition to become a teacher, her first school, to which she had to walk two miles each way, and her free Sunday school for poor children, including a class of black pupils—"little misses of color"[66]—all before she arrives in Hartford.

The pages on her school in Mrs. Wadsworth's house are mostly devoted to her teaching ideology, the scheduling of her school day, and her curriculum. Sigourney obliquely, but quite intentionally, implies that her methods followed those of Jesus, calling Alice one of her "disciples" and quoting from the Gospel of John 6:12 in explaining that her Friday reviews "gathered up the fragments," as Jesus instructed his disciples to do after his miracle of the loaves and fishes. This passage appears in her autobiography just ten pages after the passage reprinted here in part 4 on her quasi-theological arguments with "the Rev. Mr. Gallaudet" on whether her pedagogical methods or his were more consonant with Scripture. Alice is the only pupil who is discussed as an individual in this, Sigourney's last, book.

In the embedded poem, "Les Sourds Muets se trouvent-ils malheureux?" Sigourney was clearly captivated by the highly animated expressivity she observed in Alice and, later, other deaf children, and she writes that anyone who could see such children would never doubt that they are happy. Stanzas 5 and 6 repeat the conventional ideas that deaf people are (luckily) preserved from hearing "censure, pride, or art" (that is, cunning) and from speaking of "human woes." The last two stanzas develop a nice metaphor: the stream that flows silently and the stream that "bursts with torrents hoarse" both empty into the same "Eternal wave," just as deaf and hearing children both offer up their tributes to the same God.

This poem was first published as "On a Question Proposed: At the Institution of the Abbé Sicard, in Paris, 'Les Sourds-Muets se trouvent-ils malheureux?'" in Sigourney's 1827 *Poems*. It also appeared as "Answer to a Question" in *Scenes in My Native Land*, 1845.

On Friday afternoon was a thorough review of all the studies which had been pursued during the week—a "gathering up of the fragments, that nothing might be lost." Then, also, my dear little silent disciple, Alice Cogswell, the loved of all, had her pleasant privilege of examination. Coming ever to my side, if she saw me a moment disengaged, with her sweet supplication, "Please, teach Alice something," the words, or historical facts thus explained by signs, were alphabetically arranged in a small manuscript book, for her to recapitulate and familiarize. Great was her delight when called forth to take her part. Descriptions in animated gesture she was fond of intermingling with a few articulate sounds, unshaped by the ear's criticism. In alluding to the death of Henry II of England from a surfeit of lamprey-eels, she invariably uttered, in strong, guttural intonation, the word "fool!" adding, by signs, her contempt of eating too much, and a scornful imitation of the squirming creature who had thus prostrated a mighty king. Fragments from the annals of all nations, with the signification of a multitude of words, had been taught by little and little, until her lexicon had become comprehensive; and as her companions, from love, had possessed themselves of the manual alphabet and much of the sign-language, they affectionately proposed that the examination should be of themselves, and that she might be permitted to conduct it. Here was a new pleasure, the result of their thoughtful kindness. Eminently happy was she made, while each in rotation answered with the lips her question given by the hand, I alternately officiating as interpreter to her, or critic to them, if an explanation chanced to be erroneous. Never can I forget the varied expressions of intelligence, *naïveté*, irony, or love that would radiate from her beautiful hazel eyes on these occasions. It was such intercourse that suggested the following poetical reply to a question once asked in the institution of the Abbé Sicard, at Paris: *"Les Sourds Muets se trouvent-ils malheureux?"**

[1]

Oh, could the kind inquirer gaze
Upon thy brow with gladness fraught,
Its smile, like inspiration's rays,
Would give the answer to his thought.

[2]

And could he see thy sportive grace
Soft blending with submission due,

---

*"Are the deaf and dumb unhappy?" [LHS]

And note thy bosom's tenderness
  To every just emotion true;

[3]

Or, when some new idea glows
  On the pure altar of the mind,
Behold the exulting tear that flows,
  In silent ecstasy refined;

[4]

Thine active life, thy look of bliss,
  The sparkling of thy magic eye,
Would all his skeptic doubts dismiss,
  And bid him lay his pity by,

[5]

To bless the ear that ne'er has known
  The voice of censure, pride, or art
Nor trembled at that sterner tone
  Which like an ice-bolt chills the heart;

[6]

And bless the lip that ne'er may tell
  Of human woes the vast amount,
Nor pour those idle words that swell
  The terror of our last account—

[7]

For sure the stream of noiseless course
  May flow as deep, as pure, as blest,
As that which bursts in torrents hoarse,
  Or whitens o'er the mountain's breast;

[8]

As sweet a scene, as fair a shore,
  As rich a soil its tide may lave,
Then joyful and accepted pour
  Its tribute to the Eternal wave.

Untitled poem beginning "You ask 'how music melts away'" (1828)

This is the second of two unpublished poems to be found in Alice Cogswell's autograph album. Sigourney begins with a prose quotation of a question from Alice, now twenty-three, which the poem attempts to answer. Question and answer are both given in lovely visual similes, two of which were suggested by Alice herself. The prose introduction, an English translation of Alice's signed question, seems to be the earliest direct quotation of Alice to be found in Sigourney's published work, and it appears to have generated Sigourney's most visual poem in the corpus collected here.

Alice says "Why cannot you tell me how music melts away? Is it not like the *smoke*, which curls so majestically, and vanishes slowly—is it like the *waves*, which move in different shapes? Oh! is it impossible for me to have an idea of the sounds I sometimes *pant to hear?*"

[1]

You ask "how music melts away,"
And how to those who hear,
The tones of heavenly melody
Die sweetly on the ear.

[2]

Just as the rushing mighty gale
Lulls to a gentle breath__
As beauty's softest colour fades
Upon the cheek of death.

[3]

Just as a wreath of falling snow
Melts on the water's breast,__
And as the sun's last splendour wanes
Along the glowing west.

[4]

As clouds of curling smoke
Before the winds are driven,
As evening's pearly tears
Exhale and go to Heaven.

[5]

As every morning hope
Is sure ere noon to die,
As every treasure fails
But that beyond the sky.

Mrs. S.

Harford Jan[uary] 1828

"Funeral of Dr. Mason F. Coggswell" (1835)

Mason Fitch Cogswell (1761–1830)—the name usually thus spelled, with only one *g*—would have been remembered in medical and local history even had his daughter Alice not been deaf and had he not therefore been one of the founders of the first residential school for the deaf in North America. Trained in medicine during the American Revolution, he was one of the first in the new nation to perform cataract surgery and to ligate the carotid artery, and he was also instrumental in the founding, in 1824, of the Retreat for the Insane in Hartford, one of the new institutions practicing "humane" treatment of the mentally ill.

Cogswell was sixty-nine years old at his death, an old man in that time, albeit, from what this poem tells us, still vigorous. Sigourney ends the poem with Christian allusions—to King David's lyre, St. Paul's epistles, and the hospitality of Abraham ("patriarchal hospitality")—and with the prediction that the grief of the survivors will continue until *they* arrive in heaven. The single reference to the deaf population of Hartford, who apparently attended the funeral of their former classmate's father, is in the lines "while yon mute train, / Whose *speech is in the eye*," and this Sigourney has thought necessary to gloss for the national reading public.

Although the earliest publication of this poem was 1835, it is most likely that Sigourney wrote it immediately upon Cogswell's death in 1830 and that it circulated in manuscript before finding publication in her *Zinzendorff, and Other Poems*, from which this text was taken. It was later published under the title "Funeral of a Physician" in the third book she titled *Poems*, which went through many editions between c. 1841 and 1853.

FUNERAL OF DR. MASON F. COGGSWELL

There was a throng within the temple-gates,
And more of sorrow on each thoughtful brow
Than seemed to fit the sacred day of praise.
Neighbor on neighbor gaz'd, and friend on friend,
Yet few saluted; for the sense of loss
Weigh'd heavy in each bosom. Even the dirge
Breath'd tremulous—for holy music moan'd
A smitten worshipper. Grave, aged men
Bow'd down their reverend heads in wondering woe,
That he who so retain'd the ardent smile
And step elastic of life's morning prime,
Should fall before them. Stricken at his side
Were friendships of no common fervency
Or brief endurance; for at his glad tone
And the warm pressure of his hand, awoke
Fond recollections, scenes of boyhood's bliss,
And the unwounded trust of guileless years,
Glassing themselves in each congenial breast.
—The men of skill, who cope with stern disease,
And wear Hygeia's mantle, offering still
Fresh incense at her shrine, with sighs deplore[†]   [†]*weep for*
A brother and a guide: while yon mute train,
Whose *speech is in the eye*,[*] pour forth their tears,

---

[*]The deaf and dumb,—of whose Asylum in Hartford, he was a founder and patron. [LHS]

As o'er a father lost. Say,—can ye tell
How many now amid this gather'd throng
In tender meditations deeply muse,
Coupling his image with their gratitude?
He had stood with them at the gate of Death,
And pluck'd them from the Spoiler's threatening grasp,
Or when the roses from their pilgrimage
Were shorn, walk'd humbly with them 'neath the cloud
Of God's displeasure. Such remembrances
Rush o'er their spirits with a whelming tide,
Till in the heart's deep casket, tribute tears
Lie thick, like pearls. And doubt not there are those
'Mid this assembly, in the scanty robes
Of penury half wrapt, who well might tell
Of ministrations at their couch of woe,
Of toil-spent nights, and timely charities,
Uncounted, save in heaven.
                                         'Tis well!—'Tis well!
The parted benefactor justly claims
Such obsequies. Yet let the Gospel breathe
Its strain sublime. A hallow'd hand hath cull'd
From the deep melodies of David's lyre,
And from the burning eloquence of Paul,
Balm for the mourner's wound, But there's a group
Within whose sacred home, yon lifeless form
Had been the centre of each tender hope,
The soul of every joy. Affections pure
And patriarchal hospitality,
Like household deities, presiding spread
Their wings around, making the favor'd cell
As bright a transcript of lost Eden's bliss,
As beams below. Now round that shaded hearth
The polish'd brow of radiant beauty droops,
Like the pale lilly-flower, by pitiless storms
Press'd and surcharg'd. There too are sadden'd eyes
More eloquent than words, and bursting hearts;
Earth may not weigh such grief. *'Tis heal'd in Heaven.*

Excerpt on Alice from *Letters to My Pupils* (1851), including
"Excuse for not Fulfilling an Engagement" (1815) and
"Alice" (1831)

This excerpt comes from a section entitled "My Dead," in which
Sigourney provides a prose "sketch" of each of her twenty-six former
pupils who had died by the date of this book (1851) and, in some
cases, a "tribute" in the form of a poem. The sketch of Alice is the
eleventh entry in this section.

Sigourney begins her sketch of Alice by saying that "the deprivation of hearing and speech, opened for her new avenues to tenderness and sympathy," the new "avenues" being the use of facial
expressivity, which is "comprehended by all" and is an "avenue to
the soul." This passage is high praise indeed in the language of
sentimentalism, as it positions Alice as the virtuoso of "the language
of affections" and accounts for the high regard in which Sigourney
says she was held by all her classmates: she was "the darling of all."
Although Sigourney, using the diction of the time (which we also
see in the writings of, for example, Laurent Clerc) calls her deafness
a "misfortune," this passage is clearly not a play for pity—quite the
contrary, the passage is praise of Alice's extraordinary fluency in
affectional communication.

Sigourney goes on to describe Alice's intellect and "thirst for
knowledge," and to note the "considerable histrionic talent" that is
common in deaf children, though Sigourney wouldn't have known
that when she first encountered Alice. As is typical for a sentimentalist, Sigourney sees Alice's "loving heart" as the full equal of her
"fine intellect."

Sigourney's reference to a two-handed alphabet is usually taken as
evidence that a British finger alphabet chart was available in Hartford by 1815, but the alphabet in question is almost certainly the
American "old alphabet," widely printed as late as the early twentieth
century and still in use by some older Deaf Americans decades later.
Because the "old alphabet" clearly descends from the British finger
alphabet and seems to be most closely related to versions current
only in the eighteenth century, we can assume that it was known in
1815 Connecticut, although how the Cogswells or Sigourney would
have learned it is unclear.[67]

"An Excuse for not Fulfilling an Engagement" was composed when Sigourney was twenty-four, and it is one of her best poems. Her image of the Muses calling on her to inspire her composition but stopping at her schoolroom door and declining to stay for a writer who "kept a school" is a lovely expression of how the demands of a teaching job will win out over even a visit from one's Muse. "An Excuse" was published in *Moral Pieces in Prose and Verse* (1815) and in the *Miscellaneous Journal** the same year, and later as "Teacher's Excuse, Written in School" in Sigourney's *The Girl's Reading-Book* (1841) and, under slightly different titles, several more times in the late 1830s and early 1840s, and in her *Book for Girls* (1844).

The story about Alice's visit to distribute firewood to a poor family was published as a prose accompaniment to "Teacher's Excuse" in *The Girl's Reading-Book* and *Book for Girls*, and as "Be Kind to the Poor" in *The Episcopal Recorder*, 1849. Another version appeared in Sigourney's *Olive Leaves* (1852), where it was incorporated into an essay called "Silent People." As we can see in the 1841 *Girl's Reading-Book* version, Sigourney was especially proud of the charitable society that her students established, since it was their own idea and was run on their own time. The school week stretched from Monday morning to Saturday noon, leaving only Saturday afternoon for free time (since Sundays were engaged in religious observance). Yet the girls, on their own volition, gave up this precious free afternoon to come back to the schoolroom to mend old garments and knit stockings for poor families. Remembering their happy faces on these afternoons, Sigourney says they were "like a band of sisters." The "society" also collected monthly contributions from each girl, which were used to buy firewood and books. Sigourney's translation of Alice's signed narrative as given here exhibits vestigial elements of a signed-language grammar, though these were lost in the interests of idiomatic English in Sigourney's other versions of the story in which Alice's command of the language is not at issue.

---

*For more bibliographic information on magazine publications and their online incarnations, see Edna Edith Sayers and Diana Gates, "Lydia Huntley Sigourney and the Beginnings of American Deaf Education in Hartford": appendix 2.

"Alice," the poem with which this extract concludes, appeared
under the title "The Deaf Mute in Heaven to Her Friends on Earth"
in the 1834 *Poems*, as "Lines upon the Death of Miss Alice Cogswell"
in the 1839 *The Girls' Scrapbook*, and, later, in *Olive Leaves* (1852),
and, later still, as "Alice in Heaven to her Family, Left on Earth" in
The Irish Quarterly Review, 1855. In *Olive Leaves*, the poem serves
as the conclusion to a prose description of the Cogswell family by
Sigourney's friend Catharine Beecher, but everyone's name, perplexingly, has been changed, so that, for example, Alice becomes
Anna Stanley. (We say "perplexingly" because Beecher published a
similar prose description of the Cogswells, with Sigourney's poem
similarly serving as conclusion, the same year in *The Connecticut
Common School Journal*, but here with all of the Cogswells identified
by their real names.) It is a typical child elegy in the sentimental
tradition, although Alice was twenty-five at the time of her death,
an aunt to her sisters' children. You would not know that from
the poem, however, which reconstitutes the nuclear family of her
childhood. As mentioned above, Sigourney's nostalgia for the years
before her marriage when she managed not only her own life, but
also a schoolroom full of girls who adored her, must have played a
large role in her literary strategies for re-creating Alice as the little
girl she was in Sigourney's classroom.

Perhaps the most interesting thing for present-day readers about
this poem and its introduction in the immediately preceding prose
is how it establishes the myth that Alice died of grief over the death,
at age sixty-nine, of her father, Dr. Mason Fitch Cogswell. What
Sigourney actually says, however, is that Alice took to her bed and
died for the sentimentalist reason that she could not live after her
affectional bonds with her father were broken by his death, and her
own death was the only way that breach could be mended. "My heart
grew to his. . . . It cannot be separated." A less sentimentalist view
suggests that Alice succumbed to the disease that killed so many of
Sigourney's pupils and Asylum pupils like Phebe Hammond, whose
story is reprinted in part 2: tuberculosis, or consumption, as it was
then called, "that insidious disease which flushes the cheek with
beauty, while it pours deadly poison through the vitals."[68]

Alice was survived by two older sisters, Mary and Elizabeth, and
their children; a younger brother, Mason; and a younger sister,

Catherine (whom Alice calls a "rose-bud" in a sample of her English Sigourney gives here), as well as her mother. Of these survivors, Sigourney was closest to Mary and Elizabeth, who had been her pupils and with whom she kept in touch after their marriages. Yet in this poem, the three sisters are lumped together without any details that would distinguish them from one another or provide us with information about the relationship each had had with her deaf sister. Alice's brother, in contrast, addressed in the next stanza, is a distinct personality, and it seems from these lines that he was Alice's habitual playmate, the slightly younger sibling who was the companion of her early childhood. Because Mason was a boy, and hearing, he seems to have played the role of protector to his slightly older, deaf sister on their rambles about Hartford, and to have been her closest confidant. The picture of Alice and Mason's special relationship was most likely to have been accurate, given the function of the obituary poem to comfort the mourners.

The concluding two stanzas, addressed to Alice's mother, do not actually concern Mrs. Cogswell, who, as was considered proper for women in antebellum America, remains a shadowy figure here, as she does in all other surviving accounts of the Cogswell family. Instead, these stanzas describe Alice's meeting in heaven with her recently deceased father. The poem's image of Dr. Cogswell as a fond father to Alice is borne out in many family letters, and Sigourney's depiction of Alice as grateful to her father for his solicitude—to the point of "idolatry"—is surely accurate. That Alice says, in the poem, that she never realized how much she owed him until she met him in heaven would have resonated with the family and comforted them.

In this poem, we meet the stereotyped images of continuous, harmonious music played on harps and sung by an angelic choir that appear so frequently in Sigourney's work. One fresh metaphor, in the first stanza, is the notion of the melting of the wax seal that had closed Alice's ears. The seal metaphor appears in other poems by Sigourney on deaf subjects, and the depiction of deafness as a wax seal that blocks human communication was surely not very original in an age when seals on every letter had to be broken or torn away before the letter could be opened and read, but describing it as melted, rather than broken, from Alice's ear "by love divine" is a nice touch.

In the first stanza, as in "To Alice" and "For Alice," Alice wonders if she had been deaf on earth, where only "broken harmony" is heard, so that she would be more amazed—"in deeper tides of bliss"—when she heard heavenly songs. The lines, "Joy!—I am mute no more, / My sad and silent years, / With all their loneliness are o'er," seem to continue the idea, but they also refer more generally to anyone's earthly life, in which the soul is separated from heavenly bliss. Notions of life on earth as a vale of tears, a dark, lonesome valley, or metaphoric blindness remain popular today, not only in religious contexts but in folklore.

Had I been required to select from our whole number of pupils, one who drew most powerfully toward herself the unlimited regard of every heart, the selection would without hesitation have fallen upon Miss Alice Cogswell. Her peculiar misfortune—the deprivation of hearing and speech, opened for her new avenues to tenderness and sympathy. Though her tones might not reach the ear, from her eye flowed a resistless dialect, comprehended by all. The language of the affections was eminently at her control. It found a response in every bosom. To know her intimately, as it was my privilege to do, to witness the early expansion of her fine intellect, her vivid imagination, her thirst for knowledge, and her rapture in acquiring it, could not but lay the foundation of no common attachment.

Her deportment in school was most win[n]ing. Love for her teacher, and companions was ever beaming from her expressive features. The language of signs, as now exhibited in its wonderful copiousness and power, had not then crossed the ocean to this western world, to bind to society and its privileges, such multitudes of silent people. The rapid manual alphabet now in use had not reached us; and the tardy representation with both hands, of each letter constituting a word, and the few signs that we were able to invent, founded principally on visible resemblance, were, save the utterance of the eye, our only means of communication. On these, her gifted mind seized, intent to overleap every obstacle, and whenever it had possessed itself of a fact, formed rapidly its own opinions and conclusions.

Having no guide in this species of instruction, I earnestly labored to enlarge the number of signs, in which I was aided by her school-mates, for she was the darling of all. I arranged alphabetically a vocabulary of her scholastic gleanings, statedly* adding to it each new attainment, and ever when her associates had completed their weekly review of studies, she came joyfully, by the aid of this simple lexicon, to pass her own. Her definition of words, was varied by appendant descriptions, or snatches of narrative, historical, biographical, and scriptural, which had been taught her; and as she gave them by signs, her fellow-pupils in rotation interpreted orally, exulting in every acquisition or commendation, as though it were their own.

Fragments of knowledge, thus imparted and stored, she guarded as treasures, and every new idea that glowed on the mind's pure altar gave her intense delight. Each day, she was watchful of the periods of time that it was in my power regularly to devote to her; and sometimes ere the classes had quite completed their recitations, stood imploringly by my side, spelling on her slender fingers, "Have you not now something for you little Alice?" She was in a similar picturesque attitude, when the following extempore effusion, partly referring to herself, was written during the business of the school. I recollect the smiling curiosity with which she noted the rapid formation of the "short lines," as she was accustomed to designate poetry.

Excuse for not Fulfilling an Engagement

[1]

My friend, I gave a glad assent
To your request at noon,
But now I find I cannot leave
My precious charge so soon.

[2]

Early I came, and as my feet
First enter'd at the door,
"Remember," to myself I said,
"You must dismiss at four."

---

*regularly.—Eds.

[3]

But slates and books and maps appear,
　And many a dear one cries,
"Please tell us whence that river sprang,
　"And where those mountains rise,

[4]

"And when that blind, old monarch reign'd,
　And who was king before,
And stay a little after five,
　And tell us something more."

[5]

And then our darling Alice comes,
　And who unmov'd can view
The glance of that imploring eye,
　"*Oh! teach me something, too.*"

[6]

Yet who would think, amid the toil,
　(Tho' scarce a toil it be,)
That through the door the Muses coy
　Should deign to peep at me!

[7]

Methought their glance was strange and cold,
　As though it fain would say,
"We did not know you kept a school,
　We must have lost our way."

[8]

Their visit was but short indeed
　As these slight numbers show,
But ah! they bade me write with speed,
　Dear friend, I cannot go.

　　I think our silent favorite was a child of genius. Originality, and considerable histrionic talent, were early developed. I was indebted to her
for a new idea, that the hand and eye possessed an eloquence which

had been heretofore claimed as the exclusive privilege of the tongue; that the language of the speechless might find an avenue to the soul, though all unaided by the melody of sound. Her perceptive and imitative powers were also conspicuous. What she observed others do, she was anxious to attempt herself, and sanguine in expecting success. When she saw her companions addressing letters to me, she rested not until she obtained permission also to become my correspondent. Her chirography was fair and bold, for a child of nine years of age, but few, with all the obstacles by which she was surrounded, would thus have voluntarily assumed the labor of linking written speech with thought.

At first, with only a few nouns and verbs at command, she fearlessly encountered a mysterious host of auxiliaries, and connectives; and a few extracts from her letters, which I have carefully preserved, will show both her perseverance, and her improvement. One of her earliest literary efforts took the rather ambitious subject of the illumination, on the return of peace in the winter of 1815.

"The world—all peace.—Now am I glad.—Many candles in windows. —Shine bright on snow.—Houses most beautiful.—Friends at my home that night, and one baby.

"Sorry is Alice—you have no brother—no sister.—My sisters, three,—my brothers, one.—They are beautiful.—Sorry am I you never had any.—My father and my mother.—Much I love all.

"Girls, fifteen in school.—You teach.—You write, and give letters. —Cleopatra I learn—great queen—face very handsome—say to maid,—bring basket—figs—asp bite arm—swell—die.

"Xerxes, proud king—very many soldiers—go to fight Greeks—come back creeping—many men killed.

"Zones, five;—one warm, all people faint; two very cold—two half hot, half cold—temperate.

"I have see New Haven.—My sister and I.—We lived at Mrs. Hillhouse's.—I was much shaken in the awful stage.*—Beautiful houses—very many.—Peaches and apples—sweet and good.—I like

---

*A rail line connecting Hartford and New Haven was not built until 1839, so Alice traveled by stagecoach.—Eds.

ladies—Many walks.—I love very much New Haven.—I think Hartford best.—My Burgundy rose—short—red—very bright—in my garden. —My young sister pluck buds.—She rose-bud too.—I very much love my rose in garden, and my young sister.

"Mr. Gallaudet gone to Paris.—Come back with Mr. Clerc.—Teach deaf and dumb, new words, new signs.—Oh, beautiful.—I very afraid wind blow hard on Ocean—turn over ship.—Alice very afraid.—Mr. Gallaudet will pray God to keep, not drown.—Wind blow right way.—I very glad.

"Rev. Dr. Strong dead.—He—very much knowledge—great preacher. —He tell all people to love Jesus Christ.—He very much love Him.—He went to see Jesus Christ.—Everybody very much sorry.—I am, oh, very sorry—I see him no more.

"You learn me text every morning.—I tell them you every night.— Oh, beautiful.—I love you.—To-day you teach, 'Beloved, follow not that which is evil, but that which is good. He that doeth good, is of God.'"

After the system of the illustrious Sicard was brought to this country, by the Rev. Mr. Gallaudet, and Mr. Clerc, and the American Asylum for the Deaf and Dumb established at Hartford, she became one of its distinguished pupils, and the nucleus of thought and feeling, which these spontaneous efforts of childhood disclose, expanded into a varied and polished style. Yet, pleasing associations linger around the first fragmentary unfoldings of a fine intellect, and a loving heart.

Many of these mingle with her history, when she began to aid, according to her ability, the charitable society which her school-mates had instituted. It was during an uncommonly severe winter that she first accompanied the almoners on a visit of distribution. It would be scarcely possible for any child of her tender age, with all the instrumentalities of speech, to have uttered a more eloquent description, than she gave me at her return, in her silent dialect of the hand and eye.

"We entered a little upper room. The stairs were dark and broken. We had walked through deep snows. My feet were very cold. But there was not fire to warm them. No. I could have held in one small hand, those few, faint coals. Neither was there any wood. No.

"The poor woman lay in a low bed. Half sitting up, she shivered, for she wore only old, thin garments.

"And she had a sick baby. It was pale and threw its arms about. I think it cried. But there was no doctor there. No, none.

"The father came in. He had in his hand a few pieces of pine. He had gathered them in the streets. He laid them on the fire. His wife spoke to him. Then he looked sorry. I asked my friends what she said. The words of the poor woman to her husband were,—'Did you bring a candle?' He answered,—'No. I have no money to buy a candle.' Then there were tears on her cheeks, as she said,—'Must we be in the dark, another long, cold night, with our sick child?'"

As she proceeded to describe the relief imparted, and the smiles that came suddenly over the faces of the sorrowing poor, a tear of exquisite feeling glistened in her eye. Not the slightest circumstance escaped her discriminating notice, for her heart was true to every generous sensibility.

Filial affection was among her prominent virtues. It was with her not only a duty but a delight, to testify gratitude, and try to serve those whose tenderness had nurtured her infancy. But peculiarly, in her love for her father, the late Dr. Mason F. Cogswell, known and remembered by so many as the "beloved physician,"* there seemed almost a feature of idolatry. Its enthusiasm gathered strength with years. When he was taken from her by acute disease, she drooped, as if bewildered by the shock of grief. "My heart grew to his," said she, in her strong language of gesture. "It cannot be separated." And in a few days her turf-pillow was by his side.

May we not imagine her, from a higher and purer region, thus addressing the cherished objects of kindred affection?

---

*A reference to the Evangelist Luke, whom St. Paul called "the beloved physician," and an indication of Dr. Cogswell's reputation in Hartford.—Eds.

[ALICE]

[1]

Sisters! there's music here;
   From countless harps it flows,
Throughout this bright celestial sphere,
   Nor pause nor discord knows.
   The seal is melted from my ear
     By love divine,
  and what through life I pined to hear,
     Is mine! Is mine!
  The warbling of an ever-tuneful choir,
and the full deep response of David's sacred lyre.
   Did kind earth hide from me
    Her broken harmony,
  That thus the melodies of heaven might roll,
And whelm in deeper tides of bliss, my rapt, my wondering soul?

[2]

Joy! I am mute no more,
   My sad and silent years
With all their loneliness are o'er.
   Sweet sisters! dry your tears;
Listen at hush of eve—listen at dawn of day—
List at the hour of prayer—can ye not hear my lay?*
   Untaught, unchecked, it came,
    As light from chaos beamed,
  Praising His everlasting name[†]
   Whose blood from Calvary streamed,
And still it swells that highest strain, the song of the redeemed.

*s

[3]

Brother! my only one!
   Beloved from childhood's hours,
With whom, beneath the vernal sun,

[†]Praising the name of Jesus; Calvary was the site of his death.—Eds.

I wandered when our task was done,
    And gathered early flowers,
      I cannot come to thee.
Though 'twas so sweet to rest
Upon thy gently guiding arm, thy sympathizing breast,
    'Tis better here to be.
No disappointments shroud
    The angel-bowers of joy,
Our knowledge hath no cloud,
    Our pleasures no alloy,
The fearful word *to part*
    Is never breathed above,
Heaven hath no broken heart—
    Call me not hence, my love.

[4]

Oh mother! He is here
    To whom my heart so grew,
That when death's fatal spear
Stretched him upon his bier,
    I fain must follow too!
His smile my infant griefs restrained,
    His image in my childish dream,
And o'er my young affections, reigned
    With gratitude unuttered and supreme.
But yet, till these refulgent skies burst forth in radiant show,
I knew not half the unmeasured debt a daughter's heart doth owe.

[5]

Ask ye, if still his heart retains its ardent glow?
    Ask ye if filial love
    Unbodied spirits prove?
'Tis but a little space, and thou shalt rise to know.
    I bend to soothe they woes,—
    How near—thou canst not see—
    I watch they lone repose,
    Alice does comfort thee:
To welcome thee, I wait, blest mother! come to me.

Part 2

Deaf Hartford

The Connecticut Asylum for the Education and Instruction of Deaf and Dumb Persons, subsequently the American Asylum at Hartford for the Education and Instruction of the Deaf and Dumb, and now the American School for the Deaf, was the first of the state residential schools for deaf children that dominated deaf education until the late twentieth century. The story of its founding has been told in fascinating detail by Harlan Lane in *When the Mind Hears* and, more succinctly, by John V. Van Cleve and Barry A. Crouch in *A Place of Their Own.*

Beginning in 1812, Dr. Mason Fitch Cogswell and Sylvester Gilbert, a lawyer and father of five deaf children, worked on plans to convince the Connecticut state legislature to provide financial support for the school. Because the notion of petitioning a state legislature to support a school of any sort was without precedent, Cogswell also embarked on a campaign of soliciting cash donations from wealthy New Englanders, promising membership on the school's board of directors to anyone who gave at least $100. This was how the importer and wholesale merchant Charles Sigourney came to his membership on that board. Once Gallaudet had returned from his European trip, bringing Clerc back with him to establish the school, the job of raising money passed to the two of them. They travelled around New York and New England putting on demonstrations and, at one point, trying to block the establishment of a rival school in New York City (which opened anyway, in 1818). When the Connecticut legislature finally granted the school a charter and $5,000, that much again had been raised in private donations.

In addition to establishing the precedent for state support, the Asylum also established the model for the residential school. The incidence of deaf children was too low, the United States too sparsely populated, and transportation too primitive for a permanent day school to have thrived anywhere, and it was these practical considerations that, without conscious intent, created Deaf communities: deaf people who had lived together during their school years married one another, held annual reunions, and established state associations. And these arrangements made possible the development of what is now called American Sign Language.

It is impossible now to reconstruct the signed language used in the Asylum classrooms when the school opened in 1817. Clerc brought the so-called methodical sign used in Paris, which artificially combined a Parisian natural sign lexicon with a signed grammar based on spoken French, the purpose of which was specifically to teach written French to deaf children. Clerc and Gallaudet must have altered this mode of communication considerably before they tried to use it in conjunction with English. Deaf Americans had not been sitting on their hands prior to his arrival on these shores, however, and the enrollment of pupils with deaf siblings suggests a pastiche of signed proto-languages at the school. In addition, pupils from Martha's Vineyard, which had a well-developed sign language, now lost, would naturally have arrived in Hartford signing the language they knew. In this stew, ASL was born. And it was the language, more than any other kind of shared history or experiences, that cemented the Deaf community, then and to this day.

How conscious the players were of the creation of an American Deaf community is arguable. Gallaudet left the school after thirteen years with no apparent regret to work with hearing people, not only resigning his position at the Asylum but abandoning his efforts to tutor his deaf wife to improve her literacy. We know, however, that he understood that a Deaf community was in existence in Hartford a mere twenty years after the school was founded, because he turned down an offer to work in Massachusetts in 1838 on the grounds that his wife would not find a circle of friends "who know her language" outside of Hartford.[69] Some former pupils like Alice Cogswell and John Brewster Jr., who enrolled in the first class at age fifty-one but soon returned to his life as an itinerant portraitist, lived happily, or at least quite willingly, among the hearing. Laurent Clerc stayed at the school until his death at age eighty-four in 1869, complaining bitterly about how the new pupils were mutilating his beautiful language of signs, wholly unaware that he was witnessing the birth of a new language. But the number of marriages among pupils and the rapid recognition of alumni as experts who went on to found and lead deaf schools in other states presaged the debate of 1858, carried out in the pages of the *American Annals of the Deaf and Dumb*, on the establishment of a deaf state.[70] Lydia Sigourney saw it all, close up.

Despite witnessing so many deaf boys and girls grow up into literate, self-sufficient adults, Sigourney never abandoned her sentimentalist approach to the world, her beliefs that true affection was the highest virtue and human relationship the highest good to which one could aspire on earth, and that heaven was where all deficits would be made right. And to illustrate this ideology, she continued to take deaf children as subjects for her work. What we would give today for a poem of hers on, for example, Laurent Clerc as a teacher or father, or Sophia Fowler Gallaudet as the grandmotherly "Queen of the Deaf"! But this was not to be. The poems and stories collected here nevertheless cast some welcome light on the lives of deaf children before their enrollment and on deaf pupils attending a local church, returning to their families with a signed language, and marrying another deaf person.

Excerpt on the American Asylum from *Scenes in My Native Land* (1845)

Scenes in My Native Land was one of Sigourney's contributions to what was in America an emerging genre, travel books; the other was her earlier *Pleasant Memories of Pleasant Lands* (1843) about her travels in Europe. But while the so-called Grand Tour of continental Europe had long been an established element of social polish, the notion of touring picturesque spots of the American landscape, where access roads were so poor, could not have emerged before the refinement of the steamboat after 1800, when the establishment of regular steamboat service could bring tourists upstream and inland. By the 1820s, therefore, American tourism became possible and American travel books were not far behind. One early tour took travelers from the Long Island Sound up the Connecticut River Valley, through Hartford, and into Massachusetts and even New

Hampshire; another took tourists up the Hudson River through the Catskills to Albany, then westward on the Erie Canal to Niagara. Both these tours are represented in *Scenes*. In addition to unusual or romantic scenery, common stops on these tours were the various new institutions: prisons, asylums for "the insane," and schools for deaf and blind children. Tourists visited these sites not for entertainment, as had famously motivated eighteenth-century Londoners to visit the Bedlam hospital, but rather out of genuine interest in such modern, efficient, and apparently successful establishments. That they were often built on hilltops and other highly visible sites demonstrates that their founders saw them as show pieces. This untitled essay introduced readers all over the country to the school in Hartford and its modern, spacious campus—on a hilltop at 690 Asylum Avenue, currently the site of the world headquarters of the Hartford Insurance Company.

Sigourney was not the only woman of her era writing travel literature, and the genre was not uncommon in the women's magazines. However, many readers must have found it untoward for women, whose sphere, after all, was supposed to be the "cradle, hearth-stone, and death-bed," to be writing about trips to Niagara Falls. Sigourney, for her part, justified women's travel by asserting that it "teaches the value of sympathy."[71]

Julia Brace, the deaf-blind woman who was the topic of so many of Sigourney's poems, is mentioned here, though without being named. As was Sigourney's regular practice, this essay is sandwiched between two poems, "Prayers of the Deaf and Dumb" and "Les Sourds Muets se trouvent-ils malheureux?" both reprinted elsewhere in this volume.

The American Asylum for the deaf and dumb, is a large and commodious edifice, in a commanding situation, at a short distance from the city of Hartford, in Connecticut.

It has in front a spacious area, planted with young trees; and the principal avenue of approach is bordered with flowers. In its rear are work-shops, where the pupils can obtain useful exercise for a portion of the interval not occupied in study. As all of these establishments are under the direction of experienced masters, it is not one of the slightest advantages of the Institution, that a trade may be thus readily acquired, giving the means of future subsistence.

In the building are eight recitation rooms, where the different classes, arranged according to grades of proficiency, daily assemble under their respective teachers; each pupil writing the lesson, from their dictation, upon a large slate resting its frame against the wall. The fixedness of attention which they display is usually remarked by visitants; while the regret which many of them testify when the hour of dismissal arrives, proves with what satisfaction the light of knowledge fills their long benighted minds.

In the upper story is a dormitory for boys, one hundred and thirty feet in length, and fifty in breadth, from whose windows, on each of the four sides, are splendid prospects of a rich and beautifully varied country. Under the same roof is the chapel, where, every Sunday, portions of Scripture are explained, and religious instruction given by the teachers. There, also, the daily morning and evening devotions are performed. It is touching, even to tears, to see the earnest attention of that group of silent beings, the soul, as it were, sitting on the eye, while they watch every movement and sign of his hand, who is their medium of communication with the Father of Spirits.

The Asylum is under the superintendence of a Principal, eight teachers, a steward, and matron. With regard to its course of instruction, it has been the wise policy of the Directors, "to procure the services of such men, and such only, as are willing to devote themselves permanently and entirely to this profession. It has also been their wish to hold out inducements to men of character, talent, and liberal education, which should lead them to engage in a life-long service. Exerting their main strength day after day in this one employment, and not having their thoughts divided by any ulterior plans of life, the chance is greater that their duties will be faithfully performed, and that the experience which they acquire, as one year follows another, in the difficult art of deaf-mute instruction, will render their services of more value to the Asylum, than those of a merely transient teacher could be expected to possess." Seven years are considered the full term for a course of education here, and it is a cause of regret that so few remain during the whole of that period.

The female pupils, out of school hours, are occupied in various feminine employments, under the charge of the matron. Gathered into the same fold, and cheered by her kind patronage, sits the deaf, dumb, and blind girl, often busy with her needle, for whose guidance her exceedingly acute sense of feeling suffices, and in whose dexterous use seems the chief solace of her lot of silence, and of rayless night.

There are at present in this Institution one hundred and sixty-four pupils, and since its commencement, in 1817, between seven and eight hundred have shared the benefits of its shelter and instruction. Abundant proof has been rendered by them, that, when quickened by the impulse of education, their misfortune does not exclude them from participating in the active pursuits and satisfactions of life. By recurring to their history, after their separation from the Asylum, we find among them, farmers and mechanics, artists and seamen, teachers of deaf mutes in various and distant institutions, and what might at first view seem incompatible with their situation, a merchant's clerk, the editor of a newspaper, a post-master, and county-recorder in one of our far Western States, and a clerk in the Treasury Department at Washington.

More than one hundred of the pupils from this Asylum have entered into the matrimonial relation; and some, within the range of our own intimacy, might be adduced as bright examples of both conjugal and parental duty.

One of its most interesting members, who entered at its first organization, and remained during the full course of seven years, was a daughter of the late Dr. Mason F. Cogswell, who was early called to follow her lamented father to the tomb. Her genius, her entire loveliness of disposition, and the happiness of her joyous childhood, caused the following reply to be made to a question originally proposed at the Institution for the deaf and dumb in Paris [. . .].

"To Fanny" (n.d.)

This undated poem to an unidentified "Fanny" was never published: a photocopy of the manuscript, in Sigourney's hand, is held by the Gallaudet Archives (Eastman, box 5, folder 10). There is no location given for the manuscript.

The first stanza of this short poem provides the typical sentimentalist view that "affections" created ideas—"fount[s] of thought"—in the deaf girl's mind. The second, and final, stanza suggests that Fanny is dying, though we probably should not take that literally, since sentimentalists always bore in mind that we all face death. Here, Sigourney returns to her well-worn notion of the joy that a deaf person will experience when the first thing she hears, after death, is the song of the heavenly hosts.

> **To Fanny**
>
> The silent lip is thine, -
>   The ear divorc'd from sound, -
> Yet many a tuneful fount of thought
>   Is in thy nature found, -
> Deep melodies are there, -
>   By sweet affections wove, -
> And angels teach thee in thy dreams
>   Their dialect of love. -
>
> So, - pure in heart pass on, -
>   Seeking thy Saviour's clime, -
> But who the rapturous joy can paint,
>   The extasy, sublime,
> When on thy soul shall burst
>   Where skies unclouded shine
> The glorious song thou <u>first</u> shall hear
>   The speech thou <u>first</u> shall join.
>
>   L. H. Sigourney

"Opinions of the Uneducated Deaf and Dumb" (1827)

The ideas in this poem, and in the 1835 story "The Mute Boy" (see p. 111), are taken from an anonymous essay that was printed in the

Asylum's Eighth Annual Report (for 1824), from which Sigourney quotes in her prose introduction to the poem. Though Sigourney does not say so, that source essay was composed by a twenty-seven-year-old woman who had been a pupil at the Asylum. This young woman's essay is reprinted here, because it gives us a rare chance to see how Sigourney used her deaf source.

BY A YOUNG LADY 27 YEARS OF AGE.

WHAT I THOUGHT OF THE SUN, MOON, AND STARS,
BEFORE I CAME TO THE ASYLUM.

I wished to look at the sun which was very brilliant as the gold, but I could not see it. I thought the sun was like a man who was a soldier. He wore his crimson dress, and stood on the sun, while he governed over all mankind every day. I was much troubled by the heat of the sun. I told my sister that he was very cruel to us, and I wanted to touch him, but I was disappointed, because I was too far from him. While the sun was coming up, I pursued to catch him in the East but I could not do it. I believed that he was very artful.* I was playing in the garden in the summer without a bonnet. My friends told me that he would make me black, and I did not believe about it. There was a reason that he could make the brown cloth on the grass white. They were excited to laugh. In the afternoon the clouds began to become very black, and I considered that the sun was melted with the lightning. The thunder was heard, and I could feel it. He threw a large ball going down the sky. Then the sunset was running under the earth, and he became the moon all night. In the morning he held a large candle which was hot all day, while he was walking towards the west. I sat on the door of the house in the evening pleasantly, and I looked up the new moon going down the west. A few days ago, when I was walking alone to the neighborhood, the half moon followed me, and I did not wish her to come. I thought I was deaf and dumb, and she was very curious. The moon was full, and became the darkness in her face like a picture. I asked my friends what was the matter with

---

*cunning.—Eds.

her? They said that they did not know what. When I went to my chamber, I extinguished a candle, and was afraid of her, and I shut the windows all night, because I disliked to be seen by her. I was very anxious to take refuge. I advised her not to follow me, but she was still obstinate. When it was dark, the moon would not come up all night, and I was glad to hear of it. There were many stars in the sky which was very pleasant. Why did they stay there? I talked with my soul, and it was not necessary that they lived. I went out of the house, and I contemplated that they had large parties pleasantly in the evening. They were riding, while they held their beautiful candles with their hands. When I was a girl, I frequently went away, and was struck to look up a star which was going into fire with fear. I thought it was like a gun, and I ran and entered to call my sister to see the star. I asked her what was the matter with it? She answered that it would kill me. I was very afraid of it, and I told her that I would go away no more in the evening. I looked up the sky, and called my friends to see the milky way. I said "some body covered there with the white cloth." I truly saw a comet which was fallen from the sky, and I trembled with terror. I wondered that I had never seen it before. I expected that some nation was burned with fire in the distant country. I did not know who made these, and I was very ignorant not to think that God was a creator of the universe.

On My Views of Death, Before I Was Instructed

I was very afraid of death. I never saw a person who was dead in the town; and I did not know what was death. When I was about 9 years old, my mother was very sick, and died. Two days ago, I was much surprised that she was put into a coffin. I resolved to ask a nurse, why was she put into it? I said, "you are very unkind and cruel to her." My mother was buried in the grave. I was very sorry that many persons left her. I thought she was moving to cry for helping but they did not hear of it. I believed that she would rise to return from the grave next week, but the other person said that she would never meet me, till the day of judgment. I said "My mother should rise herself and would meet me from the grave." I told my friends that her death was deceitful to us. I could not pass the burying ground, because I was very much afraid that the bodies would rise and catch me from their tombs.

[...]

It is striking, and scarcely creditable to present-day readers, that this young woman—she would already have been twenty years old when she enrolled at the Asylum in 1817 (as she says later in her essay) and had apparently had no language at all for those twenty years—had, in her childhood, so readily personified the sun, moon, and stars and believed them to be malevolent. Such an idea must be extraordinarily rare. An anecdote from the deaf British woman who wrote as "Charlotte Elizabeth," and who related it in her 1841 memoir, has it that a deaf Irish boy she was teaching thought the moon "was like a dumpling, and sent rolling over the tops of the trees, as he sent a marble across the table."[72] And as Sigourney points out in the first stanza of the poem, other uneducated people like the "savage" and "polar native," and mentally ill people like the "maniac," see the sun and moon as beneficent—and not particularly anthropomorphized. That this twenty-seven-year-old deaf woman was intelligent enough as a child to think logically, as when she refuses to believe that the sun will darken her skin because its action on cloth is to lighten it, adds to the mystery of where she could have gotten these odd ideas about the sun and moon. In any case, it is difficult to imagine how any young adult who acquires a first language so long after the normal language acquisition years could even remember what she thought as a child. We might best read this account as her attempt, after a year or two of schooling and a few years of subsequent life as a signing deaf adult, to re-create the extreme naïveté and the constant state of anxiety that surely shaped her thoughts before she acquired language.

In stanza 2 of the poem, Sigourney makes a guess, framed as a question, about the reason for the child's paranoia, why she believed the moon to have been spying on her. The young lady's statement is frustratingly paratactic: "I thought I was deaf and dumb, and she [the moon] was very curious." Sigourney interprets this to mean that the child understood being deaf and mute to be "a cause of blame," a "deprecated shame" (that is, a shame we seek to avert), a "blemish" and "crime." This is a questionable extrapolation from her source, as is her guess that the girl fears the sun because she does not know that plants depend on its warmth. To be fair, however, the general ideas of a spying moon and a cruel sun originated with the unnamed essayist and, as noted above, are impossible to explain in any rational way.

Beginning in stanza 3 with "The world to thee / Was a deep maze" and continuing through to the end, this poem uses, nearly verbatim, stanzas 1–3 of the unpublished "To Alice" dated the previous year, 1826. It is not possible to say, from the surviving evidence, whether this long passage was originally written with Alice or the unnamed twenty-seven-year-old essayist in mind, but the line "A sister's tenderness" makes little sense in the case of the essayist, since the only thing she tells us about her sisters is that one of them told her that a shooting star was going to kill her. On the other hand, there's no obvious reason for Sigourney to have introduced "yon unmeasured orbs," the sun and the moon, into a poem about Alice. Perhaps we are best advised to read the reused lines in the two poems as arising out of a composite picture of Alice, the imagined child, and those of their classmates whom Sigourney knew before their enrollment, like the sisters Maria and Harriet Bailey from Norwich.

The text, including stanza breaks, which at some points may not have been what Sigourney intended, is from her 1827 *Poems*.

OPINIONS OF THE UNEDUCATED DEAF AND DUMB

"I thought the sun was a soldier, and that he governed over all mankind every day.—I was much troubled at the heat of the sun. I told my sister that he was cruel to us.—I believed that he was very artful.

——When I was walking alone, the half-moon followed me, and I did not wish her to come.—I thought that I was deaf and dumb,—and she was very curious.—When I went to my chamber, I extinguished my candle, and was afraid of her. I shut the windows all night, because I disliked to be seen by her.—I was very anxious to find refuge.—I advised her not to follow me, but she was still obstinate.——There were many stars in the sky which were very pleasant. Why did they stay there?—I talked with my soul.—I went out of the [h]ouse and contemplated that they had large parties pleasantly in the evening.—They were riding, while they held their beautiful candles in their hands.—*Eighth Report of the American Asylum for the Deaf and Dumb*

[1]

And didst thou fear the queen of night?
 Poor mute and musing child!—
She who with silver light
 Gladdens the loneliest wild?—
Her, the stern savage marks serene,
Chequering his clay-built cabin scene,—
  Her, the polar natives bless,
  Bowing low in gentleness
To bathe in liquid beam their rayless night,
 Her, the lone sailor, while his watch he keeps,
 Hails, as her fair lamp gilds the troubled deeps,
Cresting each snowy wave that o'er its fellow sweeps;
  Even the lost maniac loves her light,
  Murmuring to her with fixed eye
  Wild symphonies he knows not why.—
  Sad was thy fate, my child, to see
In nature's gentlest friend, a foe severe to thee.

[2]

 Seem'd she with keen intent,
 And glance too rudely bent,
  Thy secret wo* to spy?—
 Haunting thy hermit path
For what thou fain would'st hide from every eye,
 Thy bosom's burden and they Maker's wrath?—
  The ear in durance bound,—
  The lip divorced from sound,
  Seem'd to thy innocent mind, a cause of blame,
  A strange, peculiar, deprecated shame;

*woe

Nature's unkindness, thou didst meekly deem
Thy *blemish* and thy *crime*, which marr'd thy peaceful dream.
  To thee, the sun was as a warrior bold,
    Terrific,* pitiless, of sway severe,   *ter
  With fiery armour, and a car of gold,
    Tyrant of this lower sphere.—

[3]

  And when with toil his head declines,
And at his western gate his crimson banner shines,
Though thought'st some conflagrated city drank
The lightning of his ire, and into ashes shrank.
    Thou could'st not hear the sound
    From the moss-sprinkled ground,
  Where every tender leaflet tells the whispering gale
      He is my sire;
      From lowly vale
        Up to his throne of fire
    Each timid bud that blows,*   *blos
    The humblest violet and the palest rose
      Fondly left the grateful eye,
  Glittering with dewy tears, or bright with rainbow die.* *dye
Thou knew'st not that the drooping plant revives
At his paternal smile, and in his mercy lives,
Nor that the earth, her vernal warmth restored,
Blossoms at his embrace, and hails her genial lord.

[4]

Thou with the sparkling stars did'st converse hold,
      Which to thy wondering sight,
  Were as gay creatures form'd of earthly mould
      Who revel through the sleepless night,
        Each holding to her sister's eye
          Her flambeau bright,
        And riding joyous through the sky
          On steeds of light;—
        Till creeping dawn like beldame grey,
          Dimm'd their zones, and roused the day.

Being of lonely thought!—The world to thee
  Was a deep maze,—and all things moving on
In darkness and in mystery.—But *He*
  Who made these beauteous forms which fade anon,
What was He?—From thy brow the roses fled,
At that eternal question, fathomless and dread.—

[5]

Yet childhood's bliss was in thine eye,
And over thy features gay would rove
  That eloquent sensibility
    Which wakens love.
  A mother's fond caress,
  A sister's tenderness,
Bade through the breast full tides of pleasure run;
  A father's prayer would bless
  His dear and voiceless one,—
Yet pensive bending o'er thy sleeping bed
For thee, their mingled tears in sympathy were shed.

[6]

Oh! snatch'd from ignorance and pain,
  And taught with seraph eye
At yon unmeasured orbs to gaze,
And trace amid their quenchless blaze
  Thy own high destiny;
Forever bless the hands that burst thy chain,
And led thy doubtful steps to Learning's hallow'd fane.*   *temple

[7]

Though from thy guarded portal press
No word of gratitude or tenderness,
In the starting tear,—the glowing cheek
  With tuneful tongue the *soul* can speak,
    Her tone is in the sigh,
    Her language in the eye,
  Her voice of harmony, a life of praise,
Well understood by *Him* who notes our secret ways.

"Prayers of the Deaf and Dumb" (1828)

This poem, given here in its 1845 incarnation, had first been published in the *Ladies' Magazine* in 1828 under the title "The Deaf and Dumb at Prayer." Because the subject is a group of deaf people ("yon mute train") observed by the hearing, the poem may well have been inspired by the sight of Laurent Clerc and the Asylum's pupils filing into Sunday service at the Episcopal church to which Sigourney belonged.

Sigourney, a Congregationalist, apparently never felt completely at home in her husband's Episcopal church (which she joined, as a matter of course, upon their marriage), writing hymns for Methodist and Presbyterian hymnals that never appeared in any Episcopal publication. Clerc, for his part, turned to the Episcopal church as the best among bad choices in a city in which there were no Roman Catholic priests. As for the deaf pupils, they would have been able to follow what was said in an Episcopal Sunday service by reading along in the Book of Common Prayer, which printed out the liturgy for every type of service. Without sign-language interpreters, the less-structured Sunday service in churches of other denominations would have been all but meaningless to deaf congregants.

Sigourney begins the poem by saying that if we are touched by seeing children pray, how much more affected we are by the sight of deaf children who "Pour forth the soul to God" though they are not able to speak with their fellow man. To be deaf is described in terms of "affliction" and as a deprivation of words to clothe their thoughts, yet, she says, the "spirit's sigh" reaches God just as quickly as do spoken words. Beginning in stanza 7, Sigourney turns the tables on readers who have begun to pity the deaf, suggesting it is "better to commune with Heaven," for which no language is needed, than with "kindred clay," fellow human beings who are spoken-language-dependent. Further, the spirit's flight to God can become "clogged" with "the pomp of words." So, she concludes in true sentimentalist fashion, loss of hearing is a gain in closer communion with God, and those who pity the deaf are mistaken.

The text is from the 1845 *Scenes in My Native Land.*

PRAYERS OF THE DEAF AND DUMB

[1]

If sweet it is to see the babe
  Kneel by its mother's side,
And lisp its brief and holy prayer,
  At hush of eventide,—

[2]

And sweet to mark the blooming youth
  'Neath morning's purple ray,
Breathe incense of the heart to Him,
  Who ruleth night and day,—

[3]

How doth the bosom's secret pulse
  With strong emotion swell,
And tender pitying thoughts awake,
  Which language may not tell,—

[4]

When yon mute train who meekly bow
  Beneath affliction's rod,
Whose lip no utterance hath for man,
  Pour forth the soul to God.

[5]

They have no garment for the thought
  That spring to meet its Sire,
No tone to flush the glowing cheek,
  Or fan Devotion's fire;

[6]

Yet upward to the Eternal Throne
  The spirit's *sigh* may soar,
As sure as if the wing of speech
  Its hallowed burden bore.

[7]

Were language theirs, perchance their tale
  Of treasured grief or fear,
Might cold or unresponsive fall
  Even on a brother's ear,—

[8]

So may they grave* upon their minds   *engrave
  In youth's unfolding day,
'Tis better to commune with Heaven
  Than with their kindred clay.

[9]

The pomp of words may sometimes clog
  The ethereal spirit's flight,
But in the silence of their souls
  Burns one long Sabbath light,—

[10]

If God doth in that temple dwell,
  Their fancied loss is gain;
Ye perfect listeners to His voice!
  Say, is our pity vain?*   *pointless

Memoir of Phebe P. Hammond, a Pupil at the American Asylum at Hartford (1833), including an untitled poem about Phebe Hammond in heaven

This brief memoir of a heartbreakingly brief life of twelve years devotes far more pages to little Phebe's death from tuberculosis than it does to her life. Passing lightly over the physical suffering of tuberculosis, Sigourney provides the details of Phebe's mental suffering, as she worries and prays every day, alone in a separate room, for forgiveness of her sins. Gallaudet's letter to the dying child, telling her in no uncertain terms "Perhaps you will die" and urging her on to further prayer for forgiveness, will be particularly shocking to many present-day readers, who may wonder what sorts of sins a twelve-year-old deaf girl could have committed that would warrant such attention. But these passages reflect the belief, common in Protestant New England at the time, in the Christian doctrine of Original Sin, which has it that every human being is born with a sinful nature inherited from Adam, and that the only remedy is salvation through Jesus Christ. Indeed, the chief purpose in educating deaf children, in the eyes of both Gallaudet and Sigourney, was to bring them to seek Jesus as their personal savior who would cleanse them of the sin with which they were born.

Much of the interest for present-day readers will be in the relationship between the two deaf sisters from central Massachusetts, their attachment to one another being so strong that the younger sister, Frances, was allowed to enroll at the Asylum despite being underaged because the two could not bear a separation. What Sigourney saw as deeply entrenched affectional attachment certainly would have had a strong language element, as each sister would have understood, and been understood by, the other to a far greater extent than would have been the case with any other of the household members, who were all hearing. It's not surprising that little Frances would have been loath to live without her sister in that family environment. Childhood language acquisition was poorly understood in the early nineteenth century, so deaf children were kept from school, the only place most of them could learn any language, until they were ten years old, long after the normal age of language acquisition. Sigourney praises the sisters' spelling skills as better than that of hearing children of the same age, but deaf people are generally excellent spellers because they are not mislead by phonetics.

Of greater interest today are the descriptions of the girls entertaining their friends and family with the large number of signs they learned, which surely means that family members, at least the younger family members, were learning the sign language that was developing at the school—Sigourney later depicts the girls' cousin as a fluent signer. We notice, too, that all the girls' teachers and classmates have name signs, still a prominent feature of ASL. These name signs are distinctive sign lexemes given to deaf people by their

peers, traditionally by classmates in residential schools if not by Deaf
parents, and to those few hearing people with whom a deaf group
is in close contact, such as a teacher. They typically reference an
aspect of the person's appearance or a physical quirk; today, they
also usually incorporate an initial of the person's name, although this
seems to have been less common in the past. The name sign is then
used in lieu of spelling out personal names on the fingers whenever
the person is referred to in conversation. This passage might be the
earliest attestation to the use of name signs in the United States.

The concluding untitled poem is written in Phebe's voice and is
addressed to her deaf sister, Frances. It includes the usual declara-
tions of the ability to hear and speak (here, sing) in heaven, the image of the seal broken from the ear (and, here, lip), and the "silent"
life on earth made happy by sisterly affection, "Balm for the whole
lost world of sound." While usually in Sigourney's works the first
thing a deaf person hears on entering heaven is the song of angels,
Phebe promises Frances that the first thing the little girl will hear
is her older sister's welcome. In a variation on that sisterly promise, Sigourney says in the prose memoir that Phebe's hearing sister
Catharine, who died three years later, was greeted in heaven by
Phebe, whose voice Catharine was hearing for the first time only
after death. It was many more years, however, before Frances had
the opportunity to redeem that promise of hearing and speech in
heaven. According to the alumni record kept by Lewis Weld and
records of an 1850 reunion, Frances Hammond married Eldad A.
Prescott, who had also been a pupil at the Asylum, had two children,
and died in 1853.[73]

This memoir was published as a freestanding booklet in 1833. In
her autobiography, Sigourney says that it was written "at the urgency
of . . . the Rev. Mr. Gallaudet [who] argued that the depressed circumstances of the family of the departed, and the means of education
for the surviving sister, might be materially affected by the pecuni-
ary aid thus derived."[74] Sigourney retold the story five years later in
an essay published in *Youth's Magazine*, where it was entitled "Do
Your Duty to Your Brothers and Sisters" and was said to provide
"a good example to those who are blessed with the power of hearing and speech."[75] The story, in shortened form, also appeared in

Sigourney's *How to Be Happy* (1833) and was incorporated into the essay "Silent People" (in *Olive Leaves*, 1852), along with "The Mute Boy" (see p. 111) and the story of Alice Cogswell's visit to a poor family (in the excerpt from *Letters to My Pupils*, in part 1).

MEMOIR OF PHEBE P. HAMMOND,
A PUPIL AT THE AMERICAN ASYLUM AT HARTFORD

Phebe Parsons Hammond, was an uncommonly beautiful and interesting child. She was the daughter of Elisha Hammond, Esq. of Brookfield, Massachusetts, and born on the 4th of March, 1817. Her perceptions were so quick, in infancy, and her attention to every passing object so lively, that the circumstance of her being deaf and dumb, was not so much as imagined by her parents. When she was nearly two years old, this was accidentally discovered, by her not regarding a loud and sharp noise from the hammer of a mechanic. As she had never been sick, to occasion the loss of any of her senses, it was therefore apparent that she must have been deaf from her birth.

When she was two and a half years old, another daughter was added to the family, and it was soon ascertained that she also was in the same situation. The hearts of the parents mourned over the misfortunes of these two lovely children. They appeared to them, excluded by nature, from participation in the blessings of education, and the privileges of an intelligent community. That noble institution, the American Asylum for the deaf and dumb, was then in its infancy, which has since diffused the light of knowledge, and the happiness of religious truth, to so many interesting and isolated beings, and which like the Banian of the East, is striking out healthful and vigorous roots, whose "leaves are for the healing of the nations."*

---

*The Banian, or Banyan, is a type of fig tree, called "the strangler tree" for its vigorous roots. The quotation is from Revelation 22:2 and refers to a "tree of life" seen in a vision.—Eds.

The attachment of these little silent sisters soon revealed itself in the most touching and endearing forms. Phebe seemed perfectly happy when little Frances was old enough to run about, and play with her. She would lead her with the greatest gentleness, take continual care lest she should get hurt, and watch over her, as with a mother's tenderness. When they were permitted to play out of doors, if she feared any thing would harm her sister, she encircled her in her arms, to protect her, and then by her cries, solicited aid and relief from others. If she wished to climb a fence, she would first ascend it alone, trying every part of it, to be sure that it was strong; and then return and help her sister, keeping hold of her with all the strength and firmness in her power, and extending her little arms on the other side, to lift her tenderly down. It was a sight more pleasing than melancholy, to view those beautiful infants at their healthful sports upon the smooth, green grass, or under the shade of the trees in summer, supplying, as far as they could, the deficiency in nature's gifts, by the sweetest, and most cheerful affections.

As they grew older, they expressed a desire to attend school, with other children. Their cousin had charge of the school. She had always loved these little silent sisters, and they were permitted daily to attend her instructions, with the other scholars. She devoted as much attention to them as was in her power, and they soon learned to sew and to write.* Their father procured for them the manual alphabet, used in the Deaf and Dumb Asylum, at Hartford, and they were thus taught to spell many words. They were very diligent in their studies, and when visitors came to the school, they were surprized at their exhibitions of writing and needle work, which excelled all others of the same age in the school.

Information of the great benefits conferred on the deaf and dumb, by the system of instruction established at the Asylum in Hartford, had now become general. It was founded by the Rev. Mr. Gallaudet, in 1816, with the aid of Mr. Laurent Clerc, formerly a teacher in the Institution of the Abbe [sic] Sicard, at Paris. Its reputation was now confirmed, and the number of instructors and pupils greatly increased. The legislature

---

*When Sigourney says that the girls learned how to "write," it is penmanship that is meant. They were learning how to hold a pen and correctly form letters; they were not learning written English.—Eds.

of Massachusetts had made liberal provision, that its own deaf and dumb should be educated there, and the parents of Phebe and Frances, were anxious that they should share in these privileges. By application to the governor, permission was obtained for them to remain there four years, and have the expenses of their board and tuition, discharged by their native state.

In the month of May, 1827, these little girls, with their father, and the cousin who had taught and loved them, arrived at the Asylum, in Hartford. Phebe was then ten years old, and Frances only seven and a half. A regulation had been in force, that no pupil should be received under the age of ten years. Those who were younger, were considered unable to derive full benefit from their system of instruction. But to part these sisters was distressing. They had been together from their infancy, both night and day. They were dressed alike, the smile on their open countenances was the same—it seemed almost like one soul animating two bodies. They had no idea of a separate existence, or a divided pleasure. They fixed on each other the most sorrowful looks at the thought of parting. No power of language was so eloquent as their imploring looks. The law relaxed itself in their case, and they were permitted to remain together.

There were at that time 140 pupils in the Asylum. Phebe took her seat immediately among them, forgetting that she was a stranger, in her delight to learn. Little Frances was more diffident, and when her father and cousin were about to depart, the tears rolled down her cheeks in a burst of grief. But she clung to Phebe, as to a mother, and was comforted. And never for a moment was she disappointed in finding from her the tenderest sympathy and love.

They soon became cheerful and happy. They loved their teachers, and their fellow pupils. They admired the delightful situation of the Asylum, its commodious apartments, and spacious grounds. Their affectionate hearts were open to every innocent pleasure, and they were treated with a kindness by their companions which made them feel at home.

They were the youngest in the school, but they soon obtained a rank among the best scholars. They were docile and industrious, and made such progress in acquiring the language, and expressing their thoughts, that they soon were able to address letters to their parents. Their hand writing was very neat, and their orthography correct. This is more than can always be said of children of seven, or even ten years of age, who have the use of all their faculties. Perhaps the deaf and dumb, who have so many obstacles to conquer in the acquisition of knowledge, may yet possess some advantages peculiar to themselves. They lose no time in listening to, or uttering those idle things which interrupt and sometimes occupy other scholars. Hence they have a greater power of fixed attention, and what they succeed in learning, is acquired more accurately and longer retained.

Phebe, as the oldest, took the utmost care of the clothes of her little sister. She wished her to be always neat, and to have every thing in its place, and seemed as if she felt it her duty to supply as far as possible the absence of a mother. Her own wardrobe she kept in perfect order. No article could be displaced, without her perceiving and restoring it. She was very neat in her person, and careful to preserve her garments from being soiled or injured. Twice a year, at the vacations in spring and autumn. Phebe and Frances went to visit their parents. They were the delight of their friends and acquaintance, and received constant and marked attentions while at home. They entertained their young companions by the number and adaptation of their signs, having one for each of their teachers, for every pupil, and for all the persons whom they knew. Though their time was spent so happily among their friends, they were always willing to return to the Asylum at the stated time. They considered it best for them to be there, and they loved to learn.

In the April vacation of 1829, they went home for the usual period of four weeks. They had now enjoyed the advantages of education for two years, and their improvement was very obvious. They were exceedingly interesting to all who saw them. When they left their parents, to return to school, it was observed that Phebe had a slight cough. But as she had always enjoyed excellent health, nothing was thought of it. Indeed, she had never been sick in her life. It was therefore with great surprize, as well as sorrow, that her parents received a letter from her instructer, mentioning her illness, and his fears that she might not soon recover. A letter from her had arrived, a short time previous, which as it is the last that she ever wrote, and a pleasing specimen of the simple idiom which often distinguishes the composition of the deaf and dumb, it will not be inapplicable to insert.

Hartford, June 16, 1829

MY DEAR MOTHER,

I wish to write a letter. I love, and am happy to learn my books. The pupils write on the slates, in the school-room. There are now, 137 deaf pupils in the Asylum. I am affectionate to all the family. I *love God.* I love to study every morning and evening, the catechism, and dictionary. The pupils go into the Chapel and Mr. Gallaudet prays to God. I hope to go home in the vacation. Some of the deaf and dumb are sick. I am sorry for the sick and unwell. God takes care of the people who love him. The deaf and dumb love to be kind, to talk, and to be happy. I heard that father would come to the Asylum. I should be happy to have father visit the Asylum. The deaf and dumb are attentive, and improve to advantage. My love to my friends. The Red-Jacket, Indian chief, came to the Asylum. The Indian went into the school-room. The Red-Jacket travelled, and visited Maine, New-Hampshire, Vermont, Massachusetts, Connecticut, Rhode-Island, and Virginia. Frances is very well. My love to my father, brothers, and sister.

I am your affectionate daughter,

PHEBE P. HAMMOND.

Nothing is decidedly mentioned in this letter respecting her own sickness. She was of a very uncomplaining spirit. She knew that her instructer had communicated to her parents an account of her feeble health, and she patiently waited their decision, without any allusion to her own sufferings. When her father arrived he was shocked at the alteration, which had taken place in so short a time. She was so low as to be lifted in and out of the carriage, and was immediately conveyed home. Hope was still entertained that she might recover. But decided pulmonary symptoms appeared, and her sickness assumed an alarming aspect. The cousin who had taken such pains in her early education, was much with her in her time of disease and depression. She rode with her almost daily. And possessing the facility of communicating with her by signs, as well as by the manual alphabet, frequently introduced conversation on religious subjects.

Phebe still trusted that she should recover, and manifested aversion at the thought of death. She was somewhat irritable and impatient at the commencement of her disease, which was foreign from her naturally placid temper. Her cousin entreated her, by the love she bore her, to open her heart to her, to tell her what were her feelings toward her teachers and companions; and if she studied her Bible, and prayed to her Heavenly Father. With a most animated countenance, she gave repeated assurances of her happiness at the Asylum, of her respect and affection for all her teachers, and associates in school, that she was instructed to read her Bible, and pray, that she was taught we are all sinners, that Jesus Christ died to save *penitent sinners*, that our hearts are evil and wicked till the Holy Spirit makes us love God, and that God requires us to pray to him, to love him, and to be afraid of sin.

When inquired of, what was her request in her daily prayers? she uniformly replied,

"I pray that I may love God, and trust in Jesus Christ."

On September 2d, the following conversation took place between her cousin and herself.

"Does Phebe expect to recover?"

"I cannot tell."

"Who made you sick?"

"God."

"Is it right that you should be sick?"

"God is just, and good. I love God."

"Who are sinners?"

"All are sinners."

"How can we be saved?"

"Jesus Christ died to save sinners."

"Where shall we go when we die?"

"If the Holy Spirit makes us love God, we shall go to heaven."

"If we do not repent and love God, where shall we go?"

"To hell."

"What will the wicked do there?"

"They cannot see God."

"What will those do, who go to heaven?"

"Love and praise God."

"Is your heart good or bad?"

"Bad. I pray the Holy Spirit may make me good."

"Does Phebe often pray?"

"Yes, morning and evening, and when I sit up."

Her affectionate relative was cheered by this clear expression of her religious belief, and the warmth of feeling with which it was imparted. It had been previously observed that she had for some time desired to be carried to her chamber, every afternoon, between the hours of four and five, and there left alone, often until the family retired for the night. There she had been found, communing with her Father in Heaven; and by her silent language of signs, it was perceived that she was imploring pardoning mercy. How affecting the sight, one so young, so lovely, so near the tomb, on whose ear no kindred voice had ever fallen, and by whose lip no feeling had ever been imparted to her fellow-creatures, lifting up her heart in the solitude of her apartment, to Him who seeth in secret, and to whose ear the unspoken thought is audible.

Late one evening, after a long and voiceless communication, with the Father of Spirits, she called her mother, and kissed her with much affection. She told her that God was good, that she had prayed for the Holy Spirit, and repeated that passage from Isaiah, "Though your sins be as scarlet, they shall be as white as snow, though they be red like crimson, they shall be as wool." Her cousin having been prevented from seeing her, for a day or two, wrote her the following letter.

West-Brookfield, Sept. 8, 1829

My dear Phebe,

I could not see you yesterday, so I send you a line, to assure you of my love, and constant remembrance of you. When the weather is pleasant, I hope we shall ride. I hope my dear Phebe will be patient in her sickness, and remember God sees her. I pray God to restore you to health. We are all sinners. We have wicked hearts. We must pray continually to God for his Holy Spirit, to create within us a new heart, to make us love God, and Jesus Christ, who died to save us. We must love the Holy Bible, love to read how Jesus died, to save us, how kind and patient, and holy he was, how he has gone to heaven, and sends the blessed Spirit down to teach us to pray, and fit us for heaven, to spend an eternity with God. In heaven there will be no trouble, nor sickness, nor pain, but all happiness and love. I hope my dear Phebe will be very kind to her dear mother who takes such kind care of her, and pray God to bless her parents.

I hope I shall see you this evening or to-morrow morning. Dear Phebe, pray much, think of God, of Jesus Christ, and of your own heart. We must all die. That we may go to heaven, and be forever happy with our Saviour, is the prayer of your most affectionate friend and cousin.

C. P. F. W.

On the evening of September 9th, her mind was filled with exceeding joy. She seemed to have found great peace in believing, and a degree of elevated delight to which she had before been a stranger. The seed sown in silent and solitary prayer sprang up to a harvest of gladness.

"I love God," said she, in her animated language of signs, "I trust in Jesus Christ. The Holy Spirit hath made my heart holy, and I shall go to heaven. I shall take no more medicine. I wish to be with my Saviour."

She urged her father and mother, her brothers and sisters, to pray, and to serve the Lord.

"There are babes in heaven," she said, "children, and persons of every age. I have seen this in my mind: I saw it in a bright dream."

She appeared to enjoy perfect happiness, and her friends were exceedingly affected by the glorious change.

September 13th. She was very desirous to have the sabbath regarded as a day of rest from worldly care and conversation. The sacredness of that season seemed strongly impressed upon her mind. She wished her sisters to study the Bible, and to pray. Frances read, in her language of signs, a part of the third chapter of St. John. She inquired the meaning of being born again. Phebe immediately replied,

"To be sorry for sin, and to trust in the Lord Jesus Christ."

A few days after, she said,

"I am so weak, that I shall die. I pray to go to heaven. God is good. Shall I see Mr. Peet's* babe in heaven?" referring to a lovely child

---

*Harvey Prindle Peet (1794–1873) was recruited from Yale College by T. H. Gallaudet to teach at the American Asylum in Hartford, where he served from 1823 to 1831 before going on to a distinguished career as Principal, then President, of the New York Institution for the Deaf and Dumb. Peet's son Isaac married a deaf woman, Mary Toles, and served at the New York school as teacher and then principal for a total of fifty-three years. Their daughter, Elizabeth Peet (1874–1962), came to Gallaudet College

of one of her instructers, whom she loved, and who had recently died.

"I love Mr. Gallaudet," she added, "and all my teachers, and all the deaf and dumb. I pray that we may all love God, and go to heaven. I wish Frances to love God. She is my good sister."

She was much cheered by receiving the annexed letter, from the Rev. Mr. Gallaudet, to whom she was gratefully attached, and who was at that time, Principal of the Asylum.

Hartford, Sept. 18, 1829

MY DEAR PHEBE,

I am sorry to hear that you are very sick. Perhaps you may die. God is good. He has made you sick. Be patient. Jesus Christ sees you. *He* is very kind. *He* died on the cross, to save all persons who will trust in him. Trust in Jesus Christ to save you. Can you pray a little to God in your mind? Try to pray to God. Ask Him to forgive all your sins, and trust in Jesus Christ, and love God. I pray to God to bless you, and if you must die, to take your soul to heaven, to be happy with him forever. I send my love to Frances, and to your dear father and mother, and brothers and sisters. May God bless you all,

Your affectionate friend,

THOMAS H. GALLAUDET

The simplicity of the Christian faith, thus depicted by her revered instructer, was already wrought into the soul of this young disciple. "Out of the mouth of this babe, God had perfected praise."* In showing this letter to her friends, she said, "I love Mr. Gallaudet. I pray for him. I wish you to write to him. Tell him I love his letter. I am glad for it. I do trust in Jesus Christ, and pray to God in my mind. I shall go to heaven. I desire to see all the deaf and dumb there."

Toward the close of September, the sufferings usually attendant on consumption of the lungs, increased to a distressing degree. She was

---

as an instructor in 1900, became dean of women in 1910, and retired in 1951. Since Phebe died in 1829, Harvey Peet's New York career and his better-known granddaughter were far in the future when Phebe hoped to see his baby in heaven.—Eds.

*A paraphrase of Matthew 21:16.—Eds.

restless, exceedingly emaciated, without appetite, and troubled with frequent and painful fits of coughing. Her cousin pointed to that sentence in Mr. Gallaudet's letter, "*Be patient.*" She appeared to be grieved.

"I am sick," said she, "but God is good."

She asked for a sheet of engravings, containing the likeness of the Abbe Sicard, and three other distinguished teachers of the deaf and dumb. Pressing the page to her bosom, she said, "Three of these are in heaven, and one in Hartford. Mr. Gallaudet gave these pictures to me, I love all my teachers."

She then raised her weak, emaciated hands, and made signs for all the teachers, told the names of their children, and expressed her love for each. Her cousin, who had been with her constantly for weeks, mentioned a desire to go out for a few hours. Phebe objected, but of being told that a few ladies met for prayer, and would remember her, she readily consented.

"Shall they ask God to restore to you health?"

"No. I would* see Jesus."

"Shall they pray that you may soon die?"

"Yes; and go to heaven."

The closing hour now drew nigh, when she who "would see Jesus," was about to close her eyes upon earthly things. She seemed gradually sinking. Her nerves became shrinkingly susceptible, so that, notwithstanding her deafness, noise, or loud speaking gave pain to her head, and especially to the region about the right ear. Those ears were soon to be freed from nature's seal, and fitted for the melodies of a more exalted clime. She still spoke of the goodness of her Heavenly Father, and of her desire to die, and go to him.

On the last afternoon of her life, October 5th, the Rev. Mr. Fowler called, and she wished him to pray with her. After he had retired, she expressed gratitude to him, and to her Heavenly Father. In the evening, the Rev. Mr. Foote called, and she desired to have prayers, soon after he entered the room. This was to be his last prayer for her on earth.

"He has often prayed with me," she said. "I love him, and God loves him."

The powers of nature continued gradually, and gently to sink, until about 20 minutes past eleven, when her spirit serenely departed, to receive the fulfillment of its wishes, and to "see Jesus." At the age of

---

*Phebe uses "would" in the now obsolete sense "want to."—Eds.

twelve, she was taken from her silent pilgrimage on earth, to the full and everlasting melodies of heaven, where the ear and lip no longer sealed, shall mingle in the strain of praises, "unto Him that hath loved us, and washed us from our sins in his own blood."*

Among the friends, who attended with the most tender care, the last sickness, and death of the subject of this memoir, was her sister, Catharine Maria, two and half years older than herself. The example of sincere trust, and heavenly happiness thus exhibited, sank deep into her heart. She earnestly sought for the same strength and hope which had been granted to her sister. She committed to writing many of the facts connected with her short life, and its peaceful termination, and at the close of this statement, added with great feeling, "What greater proof can we have of the power of God, and the working of his spirit, with the sinful heart? The deaf indeed can be made to hear, and the dumb to speak. And now my dear young friends, who may read the life and death of Phebe, is it not as important for you to be religious, as for her? Life is uncertain, but death is certain. It may come suddenly. Hear the voice of God to each one of you, 'Remember now thy Creator, in the days of thy youth.'"†

Thus awakened by the example of her sister, to seek the things that accompany salvation, she found peace in believing, and made a public profession of her faith in a Redeemer. She gave proof in her life and conversation of being a most zealous and devoted Christian. Many of her companions have reason to rejoice in her exertions for their religious welfare, and in the blessing of God on her example to them.

But her probation on earth was soon to be accomplished. She became the victim of a wasting disease, and in the month of March, 1832, passed away to the Saviour in whom was her hope, and to the sister she loved so well, and whose voice she for the *first time* heard, in the welcome at heaven's gate.

The only remaining daughter of the family is Frances, the youngest of the deaf and dumb sisters, who is still pursuing her education at the Asylum in Hartford, and evinces much intelligence, and many amiable and interesting traits of character.

---

*That is, Jesus. The quotation is from Revelation 1:5.—Eds.

†Ecclesiastes 12:1. The passage urges young people to piety while they still enjoy life, instead of turning to God only when they are too old to want to live anymore.—Eds.

May we not almost imagine the sister she so much loved, and confided in, on earth, thus addressing her from a higher mansion?

[1]

I dwell where angel-harps
    Pour forth the enraptur'd lay,*
And listen to my Saviour's tone,
    More sweet, more dear than they,—
My voice is loud among the train,
    His glorious praise that sing,
Who broke from ear and lip their seal,
    And pluck'd from Death his sting,—
Yet mid such joys, so new, so high,
For thee I bend the wishful eye.

[2]

Ah! thou art left alone
Upon the silent earth,
With whom my earliest sympathies
    and budding hopes had birth,—
Our mute and uncomplaining hours
    Serenely took their flight;
One path throughout the day we trod,
    One pillow shar'd at night;
And still I guard they lonely sleep,
And shed such tear as spirits weep.

[3]

We gaz'd upon the birds
    That soar'd on pinions high,
And wonder'd what their song could be,
    From the bright summer sky,
We might not hear the hymning choir
    That made God's worship glad;
Yet walking onward hand in hand,
    Our bosoms were not sad;
For still thy fond, confiding eye
Seem'd like a secret melody.

[4]

We saw the mother bend
  Caressing o'er her child,
And mark'd the moving of her lips
  Assuage the anguish wild,
And marvell'd in our infant hearts
  what was that mystic sway
Of language, linking thought to though,
  And charming grief away;
But in they tenderness, I found
Balm for the whole lost world of sound.

[5]

When knowledge o'er our minds
  First shed its wondrous ray,
With blended strength we gladly toil'd
    Along the shining way,
But here, its everlasting tides
  without obstruction roll,
And pour unutterable joy
  On every sinless soul;
Yet mid such bliss, I think of thee,
Sister, dearest, come to me.

[6]

Keep thou the Holy Word,
  That to thy youth was taught,
And make the Ever-Seeing Eye
  The witness of thy thought,
Invoke a Saviour's boundless love,
  To grant His Spirit free,
And at Heaven's pure and pearly gate
  I will keep watch for thee,
And the first sound thy ear shall hear,
Must be, *my welcome,* sister dear.

L. H. S.

"Marriage of the Deaf and Dumb" (1834)

This poem first appeared in Sigourney's 1834 *Poems*, and was one of her most widely reprinted poems about acquaintances in Deaf Hartford. The identity of the bridal couple is unknown, but the poem is likely a composite, since marriages among former pupils of the Hartford Asylum were common—in her essay on the American Asylum reprinted above, Sigourney says that more than one hundred former pupils had married a classmate by the time of that essay, 1845.

If the poem's statements about this wedding are to be believed, the officiate is signing the ceremony in silence and there is no spoken-English interpreting for any hearing witnesses, as would be expected today. We would assume this officiate is the Rev. Thomas Hopkins Gallaudet himself. Gallaudet had left the Asylum in the fall of 1830, intending to establish a small school for hearing children and write children's books, and in 1834 he sought, and received, ordination in the Congregational ministry, almost twenty years after completing his seminary education. It's difficult to imagine another minister in 1834 or earlier with fluency, equal to this task, in the sign language that had sprung up in Hartford.

The speaker of this poem is not Sigourney herself but rather a fictional naïve observer who thinks, "*Mute! mute! 'tis passing strange!*" and compares the minister's sign language to "necromancy," a show of magic or conjuring. The speaker's naïveté is also in evidence in the modifier "heavily" in the sentence "Methinks this silence heavily doth brood / Upon the spirit."

By the third stanza, Sigourney brings the speaker around to the understanding of the conventional Romantic notion that spoken language is inadequate for a bride's vows, which "Hath never yet been shadowed out in words, / Or told in language." Instead of ending, as she usually does, with a declaration that hearing and speech will be granted in heaven, here she concludes her poem with the thought that in heaven, the couple, still deaf, will have need only for the silent "eternal dialect of love."

"Marriage of the Deaf and Dumb" is written in blank verse, found elsewhere in this volume only in "The Funeral of Dr. Coggswell." The lines concerning the risk a young woman takes in marrying—"a maiden casts / Her all of earth, *perchance her all of heaven*, / Into

a mortal's hand"—are poignant when we consider the author's unhappy marriage to the odious Charles Sigourney, who had denied
her the separation she had asked for in 1827 and with whom she
apparently lived in an uneasy truce until his business failure in 1837
wiped out his leverage over her. This text is from the 1834 *Poems*.
"Marriage" was reprinted in Sigourney's *Pocohantas and Other Poems*
(1841), as well as in *Select Poems* (the successor of the 1834 *Poems*),
which went through at least eleven editions between 1838 and 1856,
and in her *Illustrated Poems* (1849, 1860). It also appeared as "Bridal
of the Deaf and Dumb" in Sigourney's 1850 *Whisper to a Bride*.

MARRIAGE OF THE DEAF AND DUMB

No *word! no sound!* But yet a solemn rite
Proceedeth through the festive-lighted hall.
Hearts are in treaty and souls doth take
That oath which unabsolved must stand, till death
With icy seal doth stamp the scroll of life.
No word! no sound! But still yon holy man
With strong and graceful gesture doth impose
The irrevocable vow, and with meek prayer
Present it to be registered in Heaven.
   Methinks this silence heavily doth brood
Upon the spirit. Say, thou flower-crowned bride!
What means the sigh that from thy ruby lip
Doth scape,* as if to seek some element   *escape
Which angels breathe?
     Mute! Mute! 'tis passing strange!
Like necromancy all. And yet 'tis well.
For the deep trust with which a maiden casts
Her all of earth, *perchance her all of heaven,*
Into a mortal's hand, the confidence
With which she turns in every thought to him,
Her more than brother, and her next to God,
Hath never yet been shadowed out in words,

Or told in language. So ye voiceless pair,
Pass on in hope. For ye may build as firm
Your silent altar in each other's hearts,
And catch the sunshine through the clouds of time
As cheerily as though the pomp of speech
Did herald forth the deed. And when ye dwell
Where flower fades not, and death no treasured link
Hath power to sever more, ye need not mourn
The ear sequestrate and the tuneless tongue,
For there the eternal dialect of love
Is the free breath of every happy soul.

"The Mute Boy" (1835)

This sentimentalist story pulls out all the stops: an uneducated deaf child who has lost both parents and an only sibling and is raised by an elderly blind grandmother who can neither see his signs nor convey to him the notion of the Creator. The story reuses material Sigourney had earlier developed in "Opinions of the Uneducated Deaf and Dumb" by attributing to this deaf orphan many of the notions first published in the essay by "a young lady" in the *Eighth Annual Report*. See the discussion of "Opinions," above, for that former pupil's essay. Sigourney had her story published just once as a freestanding narrative, in her 1835 *Tales and Essays for Children*, though a version of it was incorporated into "Silent People" in *Olive Leaves* (1852).

THE MUTE BOY

I will tell you about a little deaf and dumb boy, who had the misfortune to lose his father, at an early age. The bereaved mother took the kindest care of him, and an infant sister, with whom it was his chief delight to play, from morning till night. After a few years, the village where they resided was visited with a dangerous fever, and this family all lay sick at the same time. The mother and daughter died, but the poor little deaf and dumb orphan recovered. He had an aged grandmother who took him to her home, and seemed to love him better for his infirmities. She fed him carefully, and laid him in his bed with tenderness; and in her lonely situation, he was all the world to her. A great part of every day she laboured to understand his signs, and to communicate some new idea to his imprisoned mind. She endeavoured to instruct him that there was a Great Being, who caused the sun to shine, and the grass to grow; who sent forth the lightning and the rain, and was the Maker of man and beast. She taught him the three letters G O and D,—and when he saw in a book this name of the Almighty, he was accustomed to bow down his head with the deepest reverence. But when she sought to inform him that he had a soul, accountable, and immortal when the body died, she was grieved that he seemed not to comprehend her. The little silent boy loved his kind grandmother, and would sit for hours looking earnestly in her wrinkled face, smiling, and endeavouring to sustain the conversation. He was anxious to perform any service for her that might testify his affection—he would fly to pick up her knitting-bag or her snuff-box when they fell, and traverse the neighboring meadows and woods, to gather such flowers and plants as pleased her. Yet he was sometimes pensive and wept—she knew not why. She supposed he might be grieving for the relatives he had lost, and redoubled her marks of tenderness. She often perused with great interest, accounts of the intelligence and happiness of the deaf and dumb, who enjoy a system of education, adapted to their necessities, and thought if anything could separate her from her beloved charge, it would be that he might share such an inestimable privilege.

At length, the eyes of this benevolent lady grew dim through age, and when the little suppliant, by his dialect of gestures, besought her attention, she was unable to distinguish the movements of his hands, or scarcely the form of his features. It was then her earnest request that he might be placed at the American Asylum in Hartford, for the education of the deaf and dumb. There, when his first regrets at separation had subsided, he began to make rapid improvement. He became attached to his companions and teachers, and both in his studies and sports, was happy. When he had nearly completed the period allotted for a full course of instruction there—a conversation like the following took place one evening, between him and a preceptor whom he loved, viz.

"I have frequently desired to ask what were some of your opinions, before you became a pupil in this Institution. What, for instance, were your ideas of the sun and moon?"

"I supposed that the sun was a king and a warrior, who ruled over, and slew the people, as he pleased. When I saw brightness in the west, at closing day, I thought it was the flame and smoke of cities which he had destroyed in his wrath. The moon, I much disliked. I considered her prying and officious, because she looked into my chamber when I wished to sleep. One evening, I walked in the garden, and the half-moon seemed to follow me. I sought the shade of some large trees, but found she was there before me. I turned to go into the house, and advised her not to come, because I hated her. But when I laid down in my bed, she was there. I arose and closed my shutters. Still there were some crevices through which she peeped. I bade her *go away*, and wept with passion, because she disregarded my wishes. I thought she gazed at me, more than at others, because I was deaf and dumb, I feared also, that she would tell strangers of it, for I felt ashamed of being different from other children."

"What did you think of the stars?"

"They were more agreeable to me. I imagined that they were fair and well dressed ladies, who gave brilliant parties in the sky; and that they sometimes rode for amusement, on beautiful horses, while their attendants carried torches in their hands."

"Had you any conception of death?"

"When my little sister died, I wondered why she lay still so long. I thought she was lazy to be sleeping when the sun had arisen. I gathered my hands full of violets, and threw them in her face, and said in my dialect of signs, 'Wake up; wake up!' And I was displeased at her, and went to far as to say 'What a fool you are!' when she permitted them to put her in a box, and carry her away, instead of getting up to play with me.

"Afterwards, when my mother died, they told me repeatedly, that she was *dead, dead*; and tried to explain to me what death meant. But I was distressed when I asked her for bread, that she did not give it to me; and when she was buried, I went every day where they had laid her, waiting, and expecting that she would rise. Sometimes I grew impatient, and rolled upon the turf that covered her, striking my forehead against it, weeping and saying, 'Mother, get up! get up! why do you sleep there so long with the child? I am sick, and hungry, and alone. Oh, Mother!

mother!' When I was taken to my grandmother's house, I could no longer visit the grave, and it grieved me; for I believed if I continued to go
and cry there, she would at length hear me and come up."

"I know that more pains were taken to instil religious principles into
your mind, than are commonly bestowed upon the deaf and dumb. Will
you tell me what was your opinion of the Supreme Being?"

"My kind grandmother laboured without ceasing, to impress me with
reverence for the Almighty. Through her efforts I obtained some idea of
the power and goodness which are visible in the creation; but of *Him*,
who wrought in the storm and in the sunshine, I was doubtful whether
it were a strong man, a huge animal, or a vast machine. I was in all the
ignorance of heathen sin, until by patient attendance on your judicious
course of instruction, knowledge entered into my soul."

He then expressed to his teacher, the gratitude he felt for the blessings of education, and affectionately wishing him a good night, retired
to his repose.

"La Petite Sourde-Muette" (1848)

This poem was published twice in the same year, 1848, under different titles: in the *American Annals of the Deaf and Dumb*, it is given
with its French title, while in *The Friend: A Religious and Literary
Journal*, the title is rendered in English as "The Little Deaf Mute."
Why Sigourney should give the poem a French title in a publication
for teachers of the deaf is anyone's guess, but the English translation unfortunately obscures the feminine gender of the French noun
phrase, which might better be translated "The Little Deaf-Mute
Girl." The other poem with a French title reprinted in this volume,
"Les Sourds Muets se trouvent-ils malheureux?," purports to have
been inspired by a question asked in Paris, but no motivation for the
French title is discernible here.

This poem presents many of the expected sentimentalist tropes,
including that enduring figure, the hearing mother whose biggest
problem is that she will never hear her child say "Mother." There
is no indication that the subject of the poem is Alice Cogswell or
any other particular deaf child Sigourney knew, but the depiction
of the mother's thoughts and emotions is not commonly seen in

Sigourney's writings about Alice Cogswell, whose mother normally recedes into the dim background. Sigourney renders the usual closing stanzas about the deaf child being able to look forward to hearing in heaven in the usual imagery of the sealed and chained ear, and the "rapture" at the first sounds being "From the full choir of Heaven."

This text is taken from the poem's publication in the *American Annals of the Deaf and Dumb* 1 (1848, 157). It also appeared twice in *The Silent Worker*: under the title "La Sourde-Muette" in 1891 and, later, under the full French title in 1899.

LA PETITE SOURDE-MUETTE

[1]

Child of the speaking eye,—
Child of the voiceless tongue,—
Around whose unresponsive ear
No harp of earth is rung;—

[2]

There's one, whose nursing care
Relax'd not night or day,
Yet ne'er hath heard one lisping word
Her tenderness repay;

[3]

Though anxiously she strove
Each uncouth tone to frame,—
Still vainly listening through her tears
To catch a *Mother's* name.

[4]

Child of the fettered ear,
Whose hermit-mind must dwell
'Mid all the harmonies of earth
Lone, in its guarded cell;

[5]

Fair, budding thoughts are thine,
With sweet affections wove,—
And whispering angels cheer thy dreams
With minstrelsy of love;—

[6]

I know it by the smile
That o'er thy peaceful sleep
Glides, like the rosy beam of morn
To tint the misty deep.

[7]

Child of the pensive brow,—
Search for those jewels rare
That glow in Heaven's withholding hand,
To cheer thy lot of care;

[8]

Hermetically seal'd
To sounds of woe and crime,
That vex and stain the pilgrim-soul
Amid the snares of time;

[9]

By discipline made wise,
Pass patient on thy way,
And when rich music loads the air,
Bow down thy head, and pray.

[10]

Child of immortal hope,—
Still, many a gift is thine,
The untold treasures of the heart,
The gems from learning's mine;

[11]

Think!—what ecstatic joy
The thrilling lip shall prove,
When first its life-long seal shall burst
'Mid the pure realm of love;

[12]

What rapture for the ear,
When its strong chain is riven,
To drink its first, baptismal sound
From the full choir of Heaven.

Excerpts from *Sayings of the Little Ones* (1855)

These two prose depictions of deaf children are a late effort of Sigourney's. In the first anecdote, she unrealistically depicts the deaf boy as unaware of an approaching storm, which any deaf person would see, smell, and feel, and as communicating with his little hearing sister by writing on a slate, an unlikely mode of communication between young siblings, considering how quickly children invent or pick up signs. In the second anecdote, however, the hearing child's confusion of the word "sign" in its ordinary sense of a gesture or indication with the word's sense as a lexeme in a signed language is still seen today.

A little boy in the Isle of Wight, was deprived by severe sickness of the powers of speech and hearing. There were no institutions for education of the deaf and dumb, to which he could have access. But he had the blessing of a loving and pious mother, who daily devoted some time to his instruction. She taught him to write, and early imbued his mind with deep reverence for that great and good Being, who could hear the thought that prayed silently in the heart of a speechless child. The simple faith that He was near, and would protect him, gave him sweet solace.

One summer's day, a violent thunderstorm arose, and from cliff to cliff of that wild, romantic region, the peals fearfully reverberated. His sister was greatly alarmed, and at every vivid flash, threw her arms around him in terror. Knowing nothing of the uproar of the elements, he understood by her trembling, and tears, that she was greatly trouble, and running to get his little slate, wrote on it in a bold hand, and held it before her eyes,

"God is everywhere."

Two children conversed about their Sunday-school lessons, adding their own remarks and emendations.

"I think," said one, "that Zacharias, the father of John, was deaf and dumb."

"No," answered the other, "he was deprived of speech, for a time, because of unbelief. So, he called for a writing-table, and wrote the name that was to be given to his son. What makes you suppose he was deaf, also?"

"Because *he made signs*," was the quick rejoinder.

Part 3

The Deaf-Blind Girls:
Julia Brace and Laura Bridgman

L aura Bridgman (1829–1889) has been the subject of two excellent
books, both published in 2002, one by Elizabeth Gitter and the
other by Ernest Freeberg, to which interested readers are referred.
In contrast, what we know about Julia Brace (1807–1884) is little
more than what we learn from Sigourney's essay reproduced here,
which she wrote for children and which bears signs of having been
cleaned up quite a bit—according to other sources, Brace was no
saint. Another fact that Sigourney consistently omits to mention is
that when she wrote the essay "The Deaf, Dumb, and Blind Girl"
(1828) and the poem "On Seeing the Deaf, Dumb, and Blind Girl of
the American Asylum, Hartford, at a Festival" (1827), Brace was no
"girl": she was a young woman of twenty-one, and, of course, older
still when "On Seeing the Deaf, Dumb, and Blind Girl, Sitting for
Her Portrait" was published in 1834. As with Alice Cogswell, Julia
Brace perhaps remained, in Sigourney's eyes, the girl she was when
Sigourney first met her, which, in Julia's case, must have been when
she was no more than sixteen.

Julia Brace had become deaf and blind as a four-year-old, but
despite Sigourney's efforts over at least two years to secure waivers
of tuition, room and board, and a clothing allowance for her, she
was not enrolled in the Asylum until she was eighteen. Unsurprisingly at that age, she made next to no progress in her studies. Although online sources such as Wikipedia claim that Brace learned
to communicate in "tactile American Sign Language," Sigourney
states in an 1828 letter to the school's directors that, after three
years of enrollment at the Asylum, Brace was "unable to make [her
wants] known, except to a few, whose sagacity, or sympathy, have
rendered them familiar with her limited mode of communication."

In the 1828 essay reproduced immediately below, Sigourney mentions signing only to say that when Brace had to be assured that something handed to her was a gift she could keep, this was done "by a sign which she understands," suggesting that the young woman had little or no facility in the sign language evolving in Hartford but, rather, was dependent on a limited lexicon of signs standing for the small and finite number of objects and activities in what was for her a small and cloistered community. In reminiscences of Martha Dudley, the matron at the Asylum when Brace was admitted, the young woman could understand detailed instructions, such as to store her boots in a particular place and put on her shoes.[76] But this does not amount to the use of language; working border collies respond to instructions at that level, both signed and spoken. In Sigourney's poems, the notion that Brace is wholly unable to express what she is thinking is a recurring and important theme.

In 1834, Samuel Gridley Howe, who founded and headed the Perkins Institution for the Blind in Boston, visited Hartford to meet Brace, of whom he was aware perhaps from Sigourney's published writings about her. Howe wanted to make an experiment in teaching a deaf-blind child, but found Brace, then twenty-seven, far too old. Three years later, Howe located his perfect subject, Laura Bridgman, and set about teaching her English by means of, first, embossed letters and then the finger alphabet he had seen used at Hartford. In the meantime, he kept up a correspondence with Sigourney, who continued to hope he would try his methods with Brace. In a series of letters continuing into the early 1840s, Howe declares himself delighted to find in Sigourney a kindred spirit who is not shocked or saddened by deaf-blind people and, although he elsewhere expressed reluctance, professes himself eager to teach English to Julia Brace. In an 1841 letter, Howe suggests that if only Brace could meet Bridgman, she "would herself undertake to learn to talk and succeed in the attempt," the word "talk" as used by Howe meant to "talk on one's fingers"—Bridgman certainly did not speak.[77] The notion of letting Brace, now a middle-aged woman by 1840s New England standards and certainly set in her ways, be carried off to Boston for English lessons must have created some adverse reaction at the Hartford Asylum, for Howe goes on to say that "I am fearful that there would be objections made to Julia's coming, at least I have been led to think so, by some remarks made to me in Hartford." In November 1841, Howe visited Hartford again, now with Bridgman in tow, where, escorted by Sigourney, Bridgman met Brace. Howe's purpose for this visit was not to inspire Brace to talk on her fingers, but was on the contrary to demonstrate, as publicity for himself and his school, the contrast between the "animated child" he had trained and the "impassive" woman who had been trained at Hartford, thus pointing up what he believed were the "destructive effects" of signing.[78] The two deaf-blind people, woman and girl, felt each other's faces, twelve-year-old Laura gave Brace a chain she had braided; Brace, putting it in her pocket, turned and walked away. Brace did end up enrolling at Perkins the following year, where she showed as little interest in learning to fingerspell as she did in learning sign language, and she was consequently sent back to Hartford a year later, after only a month or two of instruction.

Brace continued to board at the Asylum until 1860, when she moved in with her sister. She died in 1884.

"The Deaf, Dumb, and Blind Girl" (1828)

As mentioned in the introductory remarks to this section, Julia Brace was twenty-one and had been enrolled at the Hartford Asylum for three years when this essay for children was written. The text here is that of the magazine *Juvenile Miscellany*, vol. 4, no. 2 (May 1828, 127–41). This essay was very widely reprinted, especially in children's and Christian periodicals, under titles including "Remarkable Female" and "Julia Brace," and often without author attribution. These publications include the *Christian Advocate and Journal and Zion's Herald* (1831), *Christian Register* (1831), *Christian Watchman* (1831), *Youth's Companion* (1831), *Western Recorder* (1831), and *Southern Rosebud* (1834).

Sigourney has an important insight at the end of this essay about people who have been deaf or blind from a very early age: it's not just that they do not hear or see, and have not been able to do so for a very long time, but more importantly that they have had no opportunity to store up a "treasury of knowledge" gleaned from overheard conversations between strangers or from remembered sights of people who live very differently in a city one has once visited.

The Deaf, Dumb, and Blind Girl

In the city of Hartford, Connecticut, among other interesting institutions, is an Asylum for the education of the deaf and dumb. The building is large and commodious, and finely situated upon a commanding eminence. The present number of pupils is 120, who, in different classes, and under the superintendence of several teachers, are engaged in the pursuits of knowledge. They are cheerful and happy, and enjoy their intercourse with each other, which is carried on by the language of signs, and the aid of the manual alphabet. It is peculiarly affecting to see this silent assembly offering their morning and evening prayers. Many visiters have been moved to tears, by this voiceless communion of young hearts with their Maker.

Among the inmates* of this mansion is one who particularly excites the attention of strangers. *She is entirely deaf, dumb, and blind.* Her name is Julia Brace; and she is a native of the immediate neighborhood of the Asylum. She is the only instance of so great a misfortune, of which any record is extant, except one European boy by the name of James Mitchell, concerning whom the celebrated philosopher, Dugald Stewart, published an interesting memoir, many years since in the *Edinburgh Review*. He was so irritable that few experiments could be tried for his benefit; but Julia Brace has been mild and docile, from her childhood.

She was the daughter of exceedingly poor parents, who had several younger children, to whom she was in the habit of shewing such offices of kindness, as her own afflicted state admitted. Notwithstanding her blindness, she early evinced a close observation with regard to articles of dress, preferring among those which were presented her as gifts,

---

*occupants; "mansion" is used in the British sense of a large building divided into apartments.—Eds.

such as were of the finest texture. When the weather became cold, she would occasionally kneel on the floor of their humble dwelling, to feel whether the other children of the family were furnished with shoes or stockings, while she was without, and would express uneasiness at the contrast.

Seated on her little block, weaving strips of thin bark, with pieces of leather, and thread, which her father in his processes of making shoes rejected, she amused herself by constructing for her cat, bonnets and vandykes, not wholly discordant with the principles of taste. Notwithstanding her peculiar helplessness, she was occasionally left with the care of the young children, while her mother went out to the occupation of washing. It was on such occasions that little Julia evinced not only a maternal solicitude, but a skill in domestic legislation, which could not have been rationally expected. On one occasion she discovered that her sisters had broken a piece of crockery, and imitating what she supposed would be the discipline of their mother, gave the offender a blow. But placing her hand upon the eyes of the little girl, and ascertaining that she wept, she immediately took her in her arms, and with the most persevering tenderness soothed her into good humor and confidence. Her parents were at length relieved from the burden of her maintenance, by some charitable individuals who paid the expenses of her board with an elderly matron, who kept a school for small children. Here her sagacity was continually on the stretch to comprehend the nature of their employments, and, as far as possible, to imitate them. Observing that a great part of their time was occupied with books, she often held one before her sightless eyes with long patience. She would also spread a newspaper for her favourite kitten, and putting her finger on its mouth and perceiving that it did not move like those of the scholars when reading, would shake the little animal, to express displeasure at its indolence and obstinacy. These circumstances, though trifling in themselves, reveal a mind active amid all the obstacles which nature had interposed. But her principal solace was in the employments of needle-work and knitting, which she had learned at an early age to practise. She would thus sit absorbed for hours, untill it became necessary to urge her to that exercise which is requisite to health. Counterpanes beautifully made by her, of small pieces of calico, were repeatedly disposed of, to aid in the purchase of her wardrobe. And small portions of her work were sent by her benefactors as presents to various parts of the union, to shew of what neatness of execution a blind girl was capable.

It was occasionally the practice of gentlemen, who from pity or curiosity visited her, to make trial of her sagacity by giving her their watches, and employing her to restore them to the right owner.

They would change their position with regard to her, and each strive to take the watch which did not belong to him,—but though she might at the same time hold two or three, neither stratagem or persuasion would induce her to yield either of them, except to the person from whom she had received it. There seemed to be a *principle* in the tenacity to which she adhered to this system of giving every one his own, which may probably be resolved into that moral honesty, which has ever formed a conspicuous part of her character. Though nurtured in extreme poverty, and after her removal from the parental roof, in the constant habit of being in contact with articles of dress or food, which strongly tempted her desires, she has never been known to appropriate to herself, without permission, the most trifling object. In a well educated child this would be no remarkable virtue; but in one who has had the benefit of no moral training to teach her to respect the rights of property, and whose perfect blindness must often render it difficult even to define them, the incorruptible firmness of this innate principle is truly laudable. There is also, connected with it, a delicacy of feeling, or scrupulousness of conscience, which renders it necessary in presenting her any gift, to assure her repeatedly by a sign which she understands, that it is *for her*, ere she will consent to accept it.

Continuing to become an object of increasing attention, and her remote situation not being convenient for the access of strangers, application was made for admission into the Asylum, and permission accorded by the Directors in the summer of 1825. After her reception into that peaceful refuge, some attempts were made by a benevolent instructer to teach her the alphabet, by means of letters both raise *above*, and indented *beneath* a smooth surface. But it was in vain that she punctually repaired to the school-room, and daily devoted hour after hour to copying their forms with pins upon a cushion. However accurate her delineations sometimes were, they conveyed no idea to the mind sitting in darkness. It was therefore deemed wiser to confine her attention to those few attainments, which were within her sphere, than to open a warfare with Nature in those avenues which she had so decidedly sealed.

It has been observed of persons, who are deprived of a particular sense, that additional quickness, or vigour, seem bestowed on those which remain. Thus blind persons are often distinguished by peculiar exquisiteness of touch, and the deaf and dumb who gain all their knowledge through the eye, concentrate, as it were, their whole souls in that channel of observation. With her, whose eye, ear, and tongue, are alike dead, the capabilities both of *touch* and *smell* are exceedingly heightened. Especially the *latter* seems almost to have acquired the properties of a new sense, and to transcend even the sagacity of a spaniel. Yet, keeping in view all the aid which these limited faculties have the power of imparting, some of the discoveries and exercises of her intellect are still, in a measure, unaccountable.

As the abodes which from her earliest recollection she had inhabited were circumscribed and humble, it was supposed that at her first reception into the Asylum she would testify surprize at the comparative spaciousness of the mansion. But she immediately busied herself in quietly exploring the size of the apartments, and the height of the staircases; she even knelt, and smelled to the thresholds; and now, as if by the union of a mysterious geometry with a powerful memory, never makes a false step upon a flight of stairs, or enters a wrong door, or mistakes her seat at the table.

Among her various excellencies, neatness, and love of order are conspicuous. Her simple wardrobe is systematically arranged, and it is impossible to displace a single article in her drawers, without her perceiving and restoring it. When the large baskets of clean linen are weekly brought from the laundress, she selects her own garments without hesitation, however widely they may be dispersed among the mass. If any part of her dress requires mending, she is prompt and skilful in repairing it and her perseverance in this branch of economy greatly diminishes the expense of her clothing.

Since her residence at the Asylum, the donations of charitable visitants have been considerable in their amount. These are deposited in a box with an inscription, and she has been made to understand that the contents are devoted to her benefit. This box she frequently poises in her hand, and expresses pleasure when it testifies an increase of weight; for she has long since ascertained that money was the medium for the supply of her wants, and attaches to it a proportionable value.

Though her habits are peculiarly regular and consistent, yet occasionally some action occurs which it is difficult to explain. One morning, during the past summer, while employed with her needle, she found herself incommoded by the warmth of the sun. She arose, opened the window, closed the blind, and again resumed her work. This movement, though perfectly simple in a young child, who had seen it performed by others, must in her case have required a more complex train of reasoning. How did she know that the heat which she felt was caused by the sun, or that by interposing an opaque body she might exclude his rays?

At the tea-table with the whole family, on sending her cup to be replenished, one was accidentally returned to her, which had been used by another person. This she perceived at the moment of taking it into her hand, and pushed it from her with some slight appearance of disgust, as if her sense of propriety had not been regarded. *There was not the slightest difference in the cups*, and in this instance she seems endowed with a degree of penetration not possessed by those in the full enjoyment of sight.

Persons most intimately acquainted with her habits, assert that she constantly regards the recurrence of the Sabbath, and composes herself to unusual quietness, as if of meditation. Her needlework, from which she will not consent to be debarred on other days, she never attempts to resort to; and this wholly without influence from those around her. Who can have impressed upon her benighted mind, the sacredness of that day? and by what art does she, who is ignorant of all numerical calculation, compute without error the period of its rotation? A philosopher who should make this mysterious being his study, might find much to astonish him, and perhaps something to throw light upon the structure of the human mind.

Before her entrance at the Asylum it was one of her sources of satisfaction to be permitted to lay her hand upon the persons who visited her, and scrutinize with some minuteness their features, or the nature of their apparel. It seemed to constitute one mode of intercourse with her fellow beings, which was soothing to her lonely heart, and sometimes gave rise to degrees of admiration or dislike, not always to be accounted for by those whose judgment rested on the combined evidence of all their senses. But since her removal to this noble Institution, where the visits of strangers are so numerous as to cease to be a novelty, she has discontinued this species of attention, and is not pleased with any long interruption to her established system of industry.

Julia Brace leads a life of perfect contentment,—and is, in this respect, both an example and reproof to those who for trifling inconveniences indulge in repining, though surrounded by all the gifts of nature and of fortune. The genial influences of spring wake her lone heart to gladness,—and she gathers the first flowers, and even the young blades of grass, and inhales their freshness with a delight bordering on transport. Sometimes, when apparently in deep thought, she is observed to burst into laughter, as if her associations of ideas were favorable not only to cheerfulness but to mirth. The society of her female companions at the Asylum is soothing to her feelings; and their habitual kind offices, the guiding of their arm in her walks, or the affectionate pressure of their hand, awaken in her demonstrations of gratitude and friendship. Not long since, one of the pupils was sick,—but it was not supposed that, amid the multitude who surrounded her, the blind girl was conscious of the absence of a single individual. A physician was called, and the Superintendent of the female department, who has acquired great penetration into the idioms of Julia's character, and her modes of communication, made him understand his profession by pressing a finger upon her pulse. She immediately arose, and taking his hand, led him with the urgent solicitude of friendship to the bedside of the invalid, and placing his hand upon her pulse, displayed an affecting confidence in his powers of healing. As she has herself never been sick, since early childhood, it is the more surprising that she should so readily comprehend the efficacy and benevolence of the medical profession. It would be easy to relate other remarkable circumstances respecting her, but it is not desirable that this article should be so far extended as to fatigue the reader.

Should any of you, my young friends, for whose sake this memoir has been written, visit at any future time the Asylum in Hartford, and be induced to inquire for the deaf, dumb, and blind girl, you would probably find her seated with her knitting, or needlework, in a dress, neat, and in its plainness conformable to the humility of her circumstances. There is nothing disagreeable in her countenance, but her eyes forever closed, create a deficiency of expression. Her complexion is fair; her smile gentle and sweet, though of rare occurrence; and her person somewhat bent, when sitting, from her habits of fixed attention to her work. Many strangers have waited for a long time to see her thread her needle, which is quite a mysterious process, and never accomplished without the aid of the tongue. You will perceive nothing striking or attractive in her exterior, though her life of patience, industry, and contentment, has traced correspondent lines upon her features and deportment.

My dear children, it will be difficult for you to gain a correct idea of a person perfectly blind, deaf, and dumb, even after repeatedly beholding her. Cover your eyes for a short time, and you shut out this world of beauty. Close your ears, and you exclude this world of sound. Refrain from speaking, and you cease to hold communion with the world of intelligence. Yet were it in your power to continue thus for hours, even for days, you still have within your minds a treasury of knowledge to which she can never resort. You cannot picture to yourself, the utter desolation of one, whose limited acquirements are made at the expense of such toil, and with the hazard of such continual error. Never, therefore, forget to be grateful for the talents with which you are endowed. For every new idea which you add to the mental storehouse, praise *Him* who gives you with unveiled senses to taste the luxury of knowledge.

When the smile of your parents and companions makes your heart glad, or when you look at the bright flowers and fair skies of summer, think with compassion of her, who must never see the face of her fellow creatures, or the beauty of earth and sky. When you hear the melody of music, or the kind voice of your teachers, Oh!, strive to value and improve your privileges; and while you pour forth all the emotions of your souls in the varieties of language, forget not a prayer of pity for her, who dwells in perpetual silence,—a prayer of gratitude to Him, who hath caused you to differ from her.

L. H. S.
Hartford, January 1828.

"On Seeing the Deaf, Dumb, and Blind Girl of the American Asylum, Hartford, at a Festival" (1827)

This may be Sigourney's darkest poem about a deaf person, as she considers Brace's plight, her loneliness and habitual "gloom," and the "moral night of deep despair" that the poem's speaker—and everyone else who recorded their observations of Brace—imagines must descend over her mind. Brace is shown responding happily to the scent of flowers, but otherwise laughing only when some thought or image, which she cannot express in language, comes to her mind. The concluding stanzas provide the expected promises of hearing and sight in heaven, but even these seem subdued somehow by the phrasing as rhetorical questions and by the image of a rather unsettling endless ("undeclining") day. Unlike Alice Cogswell and other deaf pupils at the Asylum, Julia Brace seemed to have had no idea of what sensory input she was missing, and thus the apotheosis lacks poignant detail and comes off as rather bloodless. That Sigourney's ideas about Julia Brace's capacity for an inner life grew more optimistic over time is shown in the two 1834 poems, below.

This poem was very widely reprinted under various titles and in various versions, with different versions not always matching the different titles, including "The Deaf, Dumb, and Blind Girl at a Festival," "The Deaf, Dumb, and Blind Girl of the American Asylum at Hartford, Connecticut," and so on. Some versions included a footnote identifying Brace; others did not. The original version from Sigourney's 1827 *Poems* is printed here. An 1835 version, appearing in *Zinzendorff, and Other Poems* and elsewhere, replaces stanzas 1–7 with a single new stanza. An 1838 version, appearing in *Select Poems* and elsewhere, simply eliminates the first seven stanzas. An 1841 version, appearing in *Pocahontas, and Other Poems* and elsewhere, replaces stanzas 1–5 with two new stanzas. Sigourney seems to have been dissatisfied with her opening stanzas and to have been tinkering with them over a couple of decades, but the last time she published this poem, in her *Illustrated Poems* of 1849, she reverted to the original 1827 version.

ON SEEING THE DEAF, DUMB, AND BLIND GIRL OF THE
AMERICAN ASYLUM, HARTFORD, AT A FESTIVAL

[1]

She sat beneath the verdant shade
　　Where young birds chirp'd in leafy cell,
Where wild flowers deck'd the mossy glade,
　　And tuneful waters murmuring fell.

[2]

And smile, and song, and mirth were there,
　　While youth and joy their tissue wove,
And white-robed forms, with tresses fair
　　Gay glided through the enchanted grove.

[3]

But there *she* sat with drooping head,
　　By stern misfortune darkly bound,
By holy light unvisited,
　　And silent mid a world of sound.

[4]

Chain'd down to solitary gloom
　　No sense of quick delight was there,
Save when the floweret's rich perfume
　　Came floating on the scented air.

[5]

She rose, and sadly sought her home,
　　Where with the voiceless train she dwelt,
In Charity's majestic dome,
　　For bounteous hearts her sorrows felt.

[6]

But while her mute companions share
　　Those joys which ne'er await the blind,
A moral night of deep despair
　　Descending shrouds her lonely mind.

[7]

For not to her, Creation lends
   Or* blush of morn,—or beaming moon,   *either*
Nor pitying Knowledge makes amends
   For step-dame Nature's stinted boon.

[8]

Yet deem not, though so dark her path,
   Heaven strew'd no comfort o'er her lot,
Or in her bitter cup of wrath
   The healing drop of balm forgot.

[9]

Oh no!—with meek, contented mind,
   The needle's humble task to ply
At the full board* her place to find,   *dining*
   Or close in sleep the placid eye,   *table*

[10]

With Order's unobtrusive charm
   Her simple wardrobe to dispose,
To press of guiding care the arm,
   And rove where Autumn's bounty flows,

[11]

With Touch so exquisitely true,
   That Vision stands astonish'd by,—
To recognise with ardor due
   Some friend or benefactor nigh,

[12]

Her hand mid childhood's curls to place,
   From fragrant buds the breath to steal,
Of stranger-guest the brow to trace,
   Are pleasures left for her to feel.

[13]

And often o'er her hour of thought,
    Will burst a laugh of wildest glee,
As if the living forms she caught
    On wit's fantastic drapery,

[14]

As if at length, relenting skies
    In pity to her doom severe,
Had bade a mimic morning rise,
    The chaos of the soul to cheer.

[15]

But who, with energy divine,
    May tread that undiscover'd maze,
Where Nature in her curtain'd shrine,
    The strange and new-born Thought arrays?

[16]

Where quick perception shrinks to find
    On eye and ear the envious seal,
And wild ideas throng the mind,
    Which palsied speech may ne'er reveal;

[17]

Where instinct, like a robber bold,
    Steals sever'd links from Reason's chain,
And leaping o'er her barrier cold
    Proclaims the proud precaution vain:

[18]

Say, who shall with magician's wand
    That elemental mass compose,
Where young affections pure and fond
    Sleep like the germ* mid wintry snows?   *seed

[19]

Who, in that undecypher'd scroll,
   The mystic characters* may see,
Save Him who reads the secret soul,
   And holds of life and death the key?

*letters
of the
alphabet

[20]

Then, on thy midnight journey roam,
   Poor wandering child of rayless gloom,
And to thy last and narrow home
   Drop gently from this living tomb.

[21]

Yes, uninterpreted and drear,
   Toil onward with benighted mind,
Still kneel at prayers thou can'st not hear,
   And grope for truth thou may'st not find.

[22]

No scroll of friendship or of love,
   Must breathe its language o'er thy heart,
Nor that Blest Book which guides above
   Its message to thy soul impart.

[23]

But Thou who didst on Calvary die*
   Flows not thy mercy wide and free?
Thou, who didst rend of *death* the tie,
   Is *Nature's* seal too strong for thee?

*Jesus

[24]

And Thou, Oh Spirit pure, whose rest
   Is with the lowly, contrite train,
Illume the temple of her breast,
   And cleanse of latent ill the stain.

[25]

That she, whose pilgrimage below
    Was night that never hoped a morn,
That undeclining day may know
    Which of eternity is born.

[26]

The great transition who can tell!
    When from the ear its seal shall part
Where countless lyres seraphic swell,
    And holy transport thrills the heart.

[27]

When the chain'd tongue which ne'er might pour
    The broken melodies of time,
Shall to the highest numbers soar,
    Of everlasting praise sublime,

[30]

When those blind orbs which ne'er might trace
    The features of their kindred clay,*   *fellow
Shall scan of Deity the face,   humans
    And glow with rapture's deathless ray.

From *Zinzendorff, and Other Poems*, 1835

This stanza replaces stanzas 1–7.

        See—while her mute companions share
            Those joys which ne'er await the blind,
        A moral night of deep despair
            Descending, wraps her lonely mind.

From *Pocahontas, and Other Poems*, 1841

These two stanzas replace stanzas 1–5.

> I saw her, where the summer flowers
> Lay sprinkled o'er the shaven green,
> While birds sang gaily from their bowers,
> And crystal streamlets flow'd between.
>
> I saw her,—but no song she heard,—
> No word of fond delight she spoke;
> Nor from the landscape's glorious charms
> One ray upon her spirit broke;—

"On Seeing the Deaf, Dumb, and Blind Girl, Sitting for Her Portrait" (1834)

This lovely poem, written when its subject, Julia Brace, was in her late twenties, was published only once and shares no lines with any other poem of Sigourney's, an unusual departure from her normal practice. The poem is addressed to the artist who is drawing Brace's portrait. We do not know who this artist was, or whether the portrait might be extant, its subject labeled "unknown," though this is unlikely since Brace's appearance is known from a later photograph. The artist is almost certainly not John Brewster, the deaf portraitist who was one of the first pupils of the Asylum, since he was not resident in Hartford after 1820.

Most of the poem draws on recycled observations about Brace, such as that her reactions to the approach of a friend or the smell of flowers were rare instances of any observable connection between events and what she was thinking. The thesis, however, is unique in Sigourney's material on Brace: that while there is no way for observers, even philosophers (today we would say "psychologists"), to know what she thought, the portraitist, with Heaven's guidance, has the skill to penetrate her mind and present it for all to see.

The text is from the poem's sole publication, in Sigourney's 1834 *Poems*.

On Seeing the Deaf, Dumb, and Blind Girl, Sitting for Her Portrait

[1]

Heaven guide the artist! Though thy skill
    Can make the enthusiast's passion tear,
And catch expression's faintest thrill,
    What power shall prompt thy pencil here?

[2]

She hath no eye—God quenched its beam,
    No ear—though thunder's trump be blown,
No speech—her spirit's voiceless stream
    Flows dark, unfathomed and unknown.

[3]

Yet hath she joys, though none may know
    Their germ, their impulse, or their power.
And oft her kindling features glow
    In meditation's lonely hour,

[4]

Or when unfolding blossoms breathe
    Their fragrance 'neath a vernal sky,
Or feeling weaves its wild-flower wreath
    As some remembered friend draws nigh,

[5]

Then doth the heart its lore reveal
    Though lip and eye are sealed the while,
And then do wildering graces steal
    To paint their language on her smile.

[6]

For still the undying soul may teach
    Without a glance, a tone, a sigh,
And well canst thou its mirrored speech
    Interpret to the wondering eye.

[7]

What though her locked and guarded mind
    Doth foil philosophy divine,
Till even reason fails to find
    A clue to that untravelled shrine.

[8]

Yet may *thine art* with victor sway
    Win laurels from this desert wild,
And to a future age portray
    Mysterious Nature's hermit child.

"Meeting of the Blind with the Deaf, Dumb, and Blind" (1834)

This poem first appeared in Sigourney's 1834 *Poems*, so if it describes an actual event, as it seems to, it must have been occasioned by Howe's first visit to Hartford to meet Brace in that same year. If so, Howe must have been accompanied on that visit by a group of his pupils, not including Laura Bridgman, of course, whom he was not to meet until 1837.

This poem is one of Sigourney's most positive in terms of attitudes toward deaf and blind children. Although she hints at "some latent evil," she begins by remarking on their "youth and health and hope." In the second stanza, which describes Julia Brace, Sigourney again remarks on her inscrutability but asks, rhetorically, whether her action of turning away might not be caused by her sympathy for the blind children! We then see both the deaf children, in stanza 3, and the blind children, in stanzas 4 and 5, rejoicing in what the senses they have, the deaf to enjoy "bright Creation's boundless store" and the blind to enjoy both music and the intellect, which shines so bright it makes the very sun look like the flicker of a glow-worm. Though

Pity had gazed in sorrow on these children so "scantly" endowed with "Nature's gifts," the children themselves are exulting in praise of their Maker, for whom they feel only gratitude. Nicely said. Sigourney ends on a preacherly note with a little dig at the hearing and sighted whose thanks for the "giver's care" is "cold" in comparison.

The text is from the 1834 *Poems*. A British editor, Jane Margaret Strickland, included it under a different title, "The Hapless Ones," in her 1838 *Sacred Minstrelsy, or Poetry for the Devout*, where the deaf-blind subject is mistakenly identified in a footnote as "Julia Price." Sigourney used this poem a second time in *The Western Home* (1854).

MEETING OF THE BLIND WITH THE DEAF, DUMB, AND BLIND

On the meeting of the blind pupils from the Institution at Boston, with the deaf and dumb, and the *deaf, dumb, and blind*, at the Asylum in Hartford.

[1]

A mingled group, from distant homes,
    In youth and health and hope are here,
But yet some latent evil seems
    To mark their lot with frown severe,
And one there is, upon whose soul
    Affliction's thrice-wreathed chain is laid,
Mute stranger, 'mid a world of sound,
    And locked in midnight's deepest shade.

[2]

And 'mid that group her curious hand
    O'er brow and tress intently stray,
Hath sympathy her heart-strings wrung,
    That sadly thus she turns away?
Her mystic thoughts we may not tell,
    For inaccessible and lone,
No eye explores their hermit-cell,
    Save that which lights the Eternal Throne.

[3]

But they of silent lip rejoiced
    In bright Creation's boundless store,
In sun and moon and peopled shade,
    And flowers that gem earth's verdant floor;
In fond affection's speaking smile,
    In graceful motions waving line,
And all those charms that beauty sheds
    O'er human form and face divine.

[4]

While they, to whom the orb of day
    Is quenched in "ever-during dark,"
Adored the intellectual ray
    Which writes the Sun a glow-worm spark,
And in that blest communion joyed
    Which thought to thought doth deftly bind,
and bid the tireless tongue exchange
    The never-wasted wealth of mind.

[5]

And closer to their souls they bound
    The bliss of Music's raptured thrill,
That "linked melody" of sound
    That gives to man a seraph's skill,
So they on whose young brows had turned,
    The warmth of Pity's tearful gaze,
Each in his broken censer burned
    The incense of exulting praise.

[6]

Yes, they whom kind Compassion deemed
    Scantly with Nature's gifts endued,
Poured freshest from their bosom's fount
    The gushing tide of gratitude,
And with that tide a moral flowed,
    A deep reproof to those who share
Of sight, and sound, and speech the bliss,
    Yet coldly thank the Giver's care.

"Laura Bridgman, the Deaf, Dumb, and Blind Girl, at the Institution for the Blind in Boston" (1838)

This poem would have been written during or soon after a trip Sigourney made to the Perkins Institution for the Blind in Boston to visit Laura Bridgman. It is, unsurprisingly, less detailed in its description of its subject than are the poems about Julia Brace. The reference in stanza 3 is to young Laura's loss of her sense of smell, which, as we've seen, played an important role in Brace's ability to identify ownership of objects and situate herself in space, and provided her with a great deal of pleasure. The closing stanzas present the conceit, in the form of rhetorical questions, that God has provided Laura with a personal lamp that cheers and guides her, but which no one else can see.

The text is from Sigourney's 1841 collection *Pocahontas, and Other Poems*, which went through at least three editions. Its first publication was in *The Christian Register and Boston Observer*, 1838, and it later appeared in *Lady's Magazine of Literature, Fashion, and Fine Arts* and *Lady's Book*.

LAURA BRIDGMAN, THE DEAF, DUMB, AND BLIND GIRL,
AT THE INSTITUTION FOR THE BLIND IN BOSTON

[1]

Where is the light that to the eye
Heaven's holy message gave,
Tinging the retina with rays
From sky, and earth, and wave?

[2]

Where is the sound that to the soul
Mysterious passage wrought,
And strangely made the moving lip
A harp-string for the thought?

[3]

All fled! all lost! Not even the rose
  An odour leaves behind,
That, like a broken reed, might trace
  The tablet of the mind.

[4]

That mind! It struggles with its fate,
  The anxious conflict, see!
As if through Bastile-bars it sought
  Communion with the free.

[5]

Yet still its prison-robe it wears
  Without a prisoner's pain,
For happy childhood's beaming sun
  Glows in each bounding vein.

[6]

And bless'd Philosophy is near,
  In Christian armour bright,
To scan the subtlest clew* that leads   *clue
  To intellectual light.

[7]

Say, lurks there not some ray of heaven
  Amid thy bosom's night,
Some echo from a better land,
  To make the smile so bright?

[8]

The lonely lamp in Greenland cell,
  Deep 'neath a world of snow,
Doth cheer the loving household group
  Though none beside may know;

[10]

And, sweet one, doth our Father's hand
    Place in thy casket* dim
A radiant and peculiar lamp,
    To guide thy steps to Him?

**that is,
Laura's
mind*

Part 4

Gallaudet

Throughout her life, Sigourney was generous to Gallaudet in her praise for his work with Alice, the Asylum, and "the insane," as well as for the books he wrote. As we have seen in the introduction to this book, Gallaudet himself had high regard for Sigourney's poetry and for her work with Alice, though the makers of his posthumous reputation did not. After their respective marriages, Sigourney probably associated more with Mrs. Gallaudet, the former Sophia Fowler, by way of her charity work than she would have with Gallaudet himself. This section concludes our book with three pieces about Gallaudet.

Excerpt on school rewards from *Letters of Life* (1866)

This brief passage explaining Thomas Hopkins Gallaudet's "system of ethics" comes from the same section of Sigourney's autobiography as the excerpt on Alice given in part 1. Gallaudet had been out of deaf education for the last twenty-one years of his life and, by the time this passage was written, dead for over a decade beyond that, but Sigourney still identifies him as the principal of the Asylum. The discussion recorded here must have occurred before he left that position in 1830.

A prominent objection to the distribution of school rewards, is the possibility of the odium of injustice. Yet there are some whose system of ethics is so delicate as wholly to discard the principle of emulation.

Of this class was my friend the Rev. Mr. Gallaudet, the accomplished principal of the Asylum for the Deaf and Dumb. Ever was he saying to me: "I dissent from your theory. You know what Book classes 'emulation' with 'wrath, strifes, seditions,' and other still more wicked works."

"Yet does not the same Sacred Volume appeal to our hope as well as our fear?—as those who run in a race for the 'prize of their high calling.'["]*

"I am sure you ought to agree with me, that a right education should teach to do right from the love of goodness, not the lucre of gain."

Our arguments, sometimes "long drawn out," usually ended in my confession of inability to manage a school without the aid of this powerful principle. I was sure that the expectation of a meed fairly earned, which would impart happiness to parents and friends, gave strength to their young hearts to overcome indolence and press on in the path of habitual duty. I felt that their guard from the dangers of competition was in the truth and warmth of their own friendships.

"A Little Girl to her Friend" (1834)

This poem was written during the years after Gallaudet resigned his position at the Asylum. In 1834, the year he was finally ordained, he was intermittently preaching at a state prison and a county jail and was turning out children's books at a rapid pace. *The Child's Book of the Soul*, which is the subject of this poem, first appeared the year of his resignation, 1830, along with *The Child's Picture Defining and Reading Book*. These were followed by *The Youth's Book of Natural Theology* (1832), *Scripture Biography for the Young* (1833), *The Child's Book on Repentance*, *The Mother's Primer*, and *The Child's Book of Bible Stories* (all in 1834), *The Every-Day Christian* (1835), and, beginning in 1840, collaborations with Horace Hooker including *The Practical*

---

*A paraphrase of The Letter of Paul to the Philippians 3:14. In this passage, Paul has been warning the Philippians against Jews who advise circumcision and, using the metaphor of a foot race in which God is the judge, telling them that, for his part, he sets his eyes on the prize, variously interpreted as grace, salvation, eternal glory, or being called to heaven with Jesus.

Spelling Book, The School and Family Dictionary, and *Scripture Biography for the Young* along with scores of contributions to journals like *The American Annals of Education, The Literary Gazette, The Quarterly Christian Spectator, Mothers' Magazine*, and, of course, the *American Annals of the Deaf and Dumb*. The poem's speaker and addressee, who has lost a sister, are not identified and are most likely notional. The text is from Sigourney's 1834 *Poetry for Children*.

A LITTLE GIRL TO HER FRIEND, WITH A PRESENT OF
THE REV. MR. GALLAUDET'S "BOOK OF THE SOUL"

[1]

Unless my mother guides my hand,
   I cannot write, you know,
But such a tide of tender thought
   Does round your image flow,
I fain must send one simple scroll
With this sweet *book about the Soul.*

[2]

'Tis written by a learned man,
   and though the size is small,
Its subject is a boundless one,
   And much concerns us all,
Because the soul can ne'er decay,
When this frail body fades away.

[3]

I've never seen this volume's power
   At all surpast,* my dear,   *surpa
For making hidden mysteries plain,
   And abstract matters clear,
Pray, let it have the highest place,
Your chosen library to grace.

[4]

I often of your sister, think,
  That early smitten flower,
Who gave her soul so cheerfully
  To God, in life's last hour:
Oh, may we meet her when we die,
In yonder, bright, unclouded sky.

"Hymn" (1851)

This elegy, composed after Gallaudet's untimely death in 1850 and read at his memorial service in 1851, was first published in Barnard's *Tribute to Gallaudet*. The portrayal of Gallaudet is squarely in the sentimental tradition of the meek, patient, self-effacing, almost androgynous man whose life was devoted to service to others less fortunate than himself. Although Sigourney and her intended audience were quite aware that Gallaudet had been trained as a Congregationalist minister and had served as a chaplain in various institutions, the poem focuses on his personal piety, not his ministry.

The first two stanzas, covering Gallaudet's work in deaf education, introduce the image of the (uneducated) deaf child as the typical spiritual orphan, isolated from family and community like a hermit or prisoner. Gallaudet is shown drawing this abject child into the world of human relationships with the gift of sign language. Notice that Sigourney's use of "speech" to mean language or communicative ability would not have been taken literally by her first readers, since speech was not taught to deaf pupils at the Hartford school.

Gallaudet's second career as chaplain at the Hartford Retreat for the Insane is introduced in the third stanza. Although neglected by Deaf history today, this phase of Gallaudet's life was well known and greatly admired in Hartford. In this poem, Sigourney distinguishes between Gallaudet's work with deaf children, in her images of contact, release, and protection, and his work with people whom we would today describe as depressed and bipolar, which involves, according to the poem, patiently bringing them to their "Healer," Jesus.

The poem concludes not with a picture of Gallaudet in Heaven but rather of the survivors mourning his death and praising God for his example. The word "urn" is used figuratively: Gallaudet was buried, not cremated.

As is typical for the sentimental elegy, the poet's personal grief at the death of her old friend is nowhere in evidence, and, in the last two stanzas, her focus is squarely on the survivors, the people whose lives Gallaudet has touched, rather than the deceased himself.

The text is from the Barnard *Tribute*. It was reprinted the same year in the *American Annals of the Deaf and Dumb* and, over the years, in a wide variety of materials created by Deaf associations for reunions and the like, where it was usually entitled "Gallaudet."

HYMN

[1]

We mourn his loss,—who meekly walked
  In the Redeemer's way,
And toiled the unfolding mind to shield
  From Error's darkening sway;

[2]

Who strove through Nature's prisoning shades
  The hermit-heart to reach,
And with philosophy divine
  To give the silent, speech;

[3]

Who 'mid the cells of dire disease
  In prayerful patience wrought,
And stricken and bewildered souls
  To a Great Healer brought.

[4]

Around his grave let pilgrims throng,
    And tears bedew his urn:
'Tis meet that for the *friend of all*,
    The hearts of all should mourn.

[5]

Yet meet it is our God to praise
    For his example here,
And for his glorious rest,—above
    The trial and the tear.

Notes

1. Kelly, *Lydia Sigourney: Selected Poetry and Prose*, 5.
2. Beecher, "Mrs. Lydia H. Sigourney," 563.
3. "The Poets of America," 209; May, *The American Female Poets*, 77.
4. Hall, "Beyond Self-Interest," 493.
5. Leonard, "A Rebel in Conservative Clothes."
6. Kelly, *Lydia Sigourney: Selected Poetry and Prose*, 15.
7. Frye, "Towards Defining an Age of Sensibility," 147.
8. Franklin, "Silence Dogood, Letter 7," June 25, 1722.
9. Petrino, *Emily Dickinson and Her Contemporaries*, 55.
10. See, for example, "Interview of the Blind with the Deaf and Dumb," *Youth's Magazine*, 1837.
11. Gitter, "Deaf-Mutes and Heroines in the Victorian Era," 183.
12. Gitter, *Imprisoned Guest*, 109–10, 7.
13. Delbanco, "This Curse of Slavery."
14. Okker, "Sarah Josepha Hale, Lydia Sigourney, and the Poetic Tradition in Two Nineteenth-Century Women's Magazines," 32.
15. Sigourney, "Essay on the Genius of Mrs. Hemans," xv.
16. Fetterley, *Provisions*, 108.
17. Olwell, "'It Spoke Itself,'" 33.
18. Quotation from Walker, *The Nightingale's Burden*, 34.
19. McGann, *The Poetics of Sensibility*, 195.
20. See, for example, Wry, "Lydia Sigourney's 'To a Shred of Linen,'" 405.
21. Olwell, "'It Spoke Itself,'" 39.
22. See, for example, Wry, "Lydia Sigourney's 'To a Shred of Linen,'" and Day, "'This comes of writing poetry.'"
23. Conrad, *Perish the Thought*, 170–71.
24. Parsons, *The Friendly Club and other Portraits*, 109.
25. Saunders, *Daniel Wadsworth, Patron of the Arts*, 23.
26. Sigourney, *Letters of Life*, 201–2.
27. Sigourney, *Letters to My Pupils*, 211, 224, 295.
28. Lane, *When the Mind Hears*, 156, 179.
29. [Dwight], Review of Mrs. L. H. Sigourney, *Letters of Life*, 347, 348.
30. Gallaudet, *Life of Thomas Hopkins Gallaudet*, 86.
31. Quotation from Gallaudet's letter to Cogswell in Lane, *When the Mind Hears*, 187; the underlining is Gallaudet's.
32. Sigourney, "Record of My School."
33. Wait, "Lydia Huntley Sigourney and Deaf Education."

34. Sigourney, Letter to the Ladies of the Directors of the American Asylum for the Education of the Deaf & Dumb.

35. Sigourney, Letter to Seth Terry, 1823 and 1828.

36. Sigourney, "Record of My School."

37. Sigourney, "Minutes for the Society for the Former Scholars of Mrs. Sigourney."

38. Sigourney, "Executive Committee of the Ladies for Greek Subscription Memorandum."

39. Day, "'This comes of writing poetry,'" 114.

40. Searing, Papers.

41. See, for example, Douglas, *The Feminization of American Culture*, and Day, "'This comes of writing poetry.'"

42. Wood, "Mrs. Sigourney and the Sensibility of the Inner Space," 175.

43. Kelly, *Lydia Sigourney: Selected Poetry and Prose*, 20, 40.

44. Wadsworth, The Will of Daniel Wadsworth.

45. Ladd, *Understanding Deaf Culture*.

46. Barnard, *Tribute to Gallaudet*, 7.

47. Ibid., 7–8.

48. Ibid., 13.

49. Weld, "The American Asylum," 132.

50. Humphrey, *The Life and Labors of the Rev. T. H. Gallaudet, LL.D.*, 29, 129.

51. Huntington, "Lydia H. Sigourney," 100.

52. Phillips, "Yale Teachers of the Deaf."

53. [Dwight], Review of Mrs. L. H. Sigourney, *Letters of Life*.

54. See, for example, Day, "'This comes of writing poetry,'"191, on the rarity of autobiographies by women.

55. Parsons, *The Friendly Club and Other Portraits*; Haight, *Mrs. Sigourney*; Lane, *When the Mind Hears*, 181.

56. Beers, "Hartford in Literature," 163.

57. Gallaudet, *Life of Thomas Hopkins Gallaudet*, 49.

58. "Note to 'La Sourde-Muette,'" emphasis added.

59. Fetterley, *Provisions*, 107.

60. Donawerth, "Hannah More, Lydia Sigourney, and the Creation of a Woman's Tradition of Rhetoric," 157.

61. Root, *Father and Daughter*, 65.

62. Walker, *The Nightingale's Burden*, 74; Dobson, *Dickinson and the Strategies of Reticence*, 94; Baym, *Feminism and American Literary History, 1790-1860*, 166.

63. Petrino, *Emily Dickinson and Her Contemporaries*, 70; Kelly, *Lydia Sigourney: Selected Poetry and Prose*, 27.

64. Roller, "Early American Writers for Children," 233; Walker, *The Nightingale's Burden*, 34.

65. Fetterley, *Provisions*, 107.

66. Quoted in Wait, "Lydia Huntley Sigourney and Deaf Education."

67. Loew, Akamatsu, and Lanaville, "A Two-Handed Manual Alphabet in the United States."

68. Sigourney, *Letters to My Pupils*, 230.

69. Humphrey, *The Life and Labors of the Rev. T. H. Gallaudet, LL.D.*, 345.

70. Flournoy, Booth, et al., "Correspondence."

71. Quoted in Imbarrato, *Traveling Women*, 122.

72. Charlotte Elizabeth, *Personal Recollections*, 75.

73. Wait, Personal correspondence to Diana Gates.

74. Sigourney, *Letters of Life*, 332.

75. Sigourney, "Do Your Duty to Your Brothers and Sisters," 232.

76. Dudley, "Letter," 30.

77. Howe, Letter to Lydia Huntley Sigourney, April 20, 1838; September 3, 1841.

78. Gitter, *The Imprisoned Guest*, 139–40.

Works Cited

"Album of Alice Cogswell." American School for the Deaf, Archives and Museum. West Hartford, Connecticut.

Barnard, Henry. *Tribute to Gallaudet.* Hartford: Brockett & Hutchinson, 1852.

Baym, Nina. "Reinventing Lydia Sigourney." *American Literature* 62, no.3 (1990): 385–404.

———. *Feminism and American Literary History, 1790–1860.* New Brunswick, N.J.: Rutgers University Press, 1992.

Beecher, Catharine Esther. "Alice Cogswell." *The Connecticut Common School Journal and Annals of Education* 6, no.3/4 (March/April 1852): 65.

———. "Mrs. Lydia H. Sigourney." *Hours at Home* (October 1865): 559–65.

Beers, Henry A. "Hartford in Literature." In *The Memorial History of Hartford County, Connecticut 1633–1884,* edited by J. Hammond Trumbull, Vol. 1, 155–74. Boston: Osgood, 1886.

Boatner, Maxine Tull. *Voice of the Deaf: A Biography of Edward Miner Gallaudet.* Washington, D.C.: Public Affairs Press, 1959.

Cavitch, Max. *American Elegy: The Poetry of Mourning from the Puritans to Whitman.* Minneapolis: University of Minnesota Press, 2007.

Charlotte Elizabeth [Charlotte Browne Phelan]. *Personal Recollections.* Abridged. Gloucester, U.K.: Dodo Press, 2006. First published London: Seeley & Burnside, 1841.

Cogswell, Alice. Letter to Thomas Hopkins Gallaudet dated July 6, 1815. Thomas Hopkins Gallaudet Papers, Gallaudet University Library Deaf Collections and Archives, Washington, D.C.

———. Letter to Thomas Hopkins Gallaudet dated August 14, 1815. Thomas Hopkins Gallaudet Papers. Gallaudet University Library Deaf Collections and Archives, Washington, D.C.

Cogswell, Mason Fitch. Letter to Harriet Cogswell dated September 2, 1815. Cogswell Family Papers. Sterling Memorial Library: Manuscripts and Archives. Yale University, New Haven, Connecticut.

Conrad, Susan Phinneg. *Perish the Thought: Intellectual Women in Romantic America, 1830–1860.* New York: Oxford University Press, 1976.

Day, Betty Harris. "'This comes of writing poetry': The Public and Private Voice of Lydia H. Sigourney." PhD diss., University of Maryland, 1992.

Delbanco, Andrew. "This Curse of Slavery." Review of *Mightier than the Sword: Uncle Tom's Cabin and the Battle for America*, by David S. Reynolds. *New York Times*, June 26, 2011, Sunday Book Review.

Dobson, Joanne. "Reclaiming Sentimental Literature." *American Literature* 69, no. 2 (1997): 263–88.

———. *Dickinson and the Strategies of Reticence: The Woman Writer in Nineteenth Century America*. Bloomington: Indiana University Press, 1989.

Donawerth, Jane. "Hannah More, Lydia Sigourney, and the Creation of a Woman's Tradition of Rhetoric." In *Rhetoric, the Polis, and the Global Village*, edited by Jan Swearingen, 155–62. Mahwah, N.J.: Erlbaum, 1999.

Douglas, Ann. *The Feminization of American Culture*. New York: Noonday, 1998. First published New York: Knopf, 1977.

Dudley, Martha. "Letter." In *Twenty-first Annual Report of the Directors of the American Asylum at Hartford for the Education and Instruction of the Deaf and Dumb*, 29–33. Hartford: Hudson & Skinner, 1837.

[Dwight, Timothy]. Review of *Letters of Life*, by Mrs. L. H. Sigourney. *The New Englander* 25 (1866): 330–58.

Fetterley, Judith. *Provisions: A Reader from Nineteenth-Century American Women*. Bloomington: Indiana University Press, 1985.

Finch, Annie. "The Sentimental Poetess in the World: Metaphor and Subjectivity in Lydia Sigourney's Nature Poetry. *Legacy* 5, no.2 (1988): 3–18.

Fisher, Philip. *Hard Facts: Setting and Form in the American Novel*. New York: Oxford University Press, 1985.

Flournoy, J. J., Edmund Booth, et al. "Correspondence." *American Annals of the Deaf and Dumb* 10 (1858): 40–68. Excerpts reprinted in *Deaf World: A Historical Reader and Primary Sourcebook*, edited by Lois Bragg, 13–26. New York: New York University Press, 2001.

Franklin, Benjamin. "Silence Dogood, Letter 7," *New-England Courant*, June 25, 1722.

Freeberg, Ernest. *The Education of Laura Bridgman: First Deaf and Blind Person to Learn Language*. Cambridge, Mass.: Harvard University Press, 2001.

Frye, Northrop. "Towards Defining an Age of Sensibility." *English Literary History* 23, no.2 (1956): 144–52.

Gallaudet, Edward Miner. *Life of Thomas Hopkins Gallaudet*. New York: Henry Holt, 1888.

———. "The American Asylum." In *The Memorial History of Hartford County, Connecticut 1633–1884*, edited by J. Hammond Trumbull, Vol.1, 425–38. Boston: Osgood, 1886.

Giffen, Allison. "Dutiful Daughters and Needy Fathers: Lydia Sigourney and Nineteenth-Century Popular Literature." *Women's Studies* 32, (2003): 255-80.

Gitter, Elizabeth. "Deaf-Mutes and Heroines in the Victorian Era." *Victorian Literature and Culture* 20 (1992): 179-96.

———. *The Imprisoned Guest: Samuel Howe and Laura Bridgman, the Original Deaf-Blind Girl.* New York: Farrar, Strauss & Giroux, 2001.

Haight, Gordon. *Mrs. Sigourney: The Sweet Singer of Hartford.* New Haven: Yale University Press, 1930.

Hall, Mark David. "Beyond Self-Interest: The Political Theory and Practice of Evangelical Women in Antebellum America." *Journal of Church and State* 44, no.3 (2002): 477–99.

Hershberger, Mary. "Mobilizing Women, Anticipating Abolition: The Struggle Against Indian Removal in the 1830s." *Journal of American History* 86, no.1 (1999): 15–41.

Howe, Samuel Gridley. Letter to Lydia Huntley Sigourney dated April 20, 1838. Hoadly Collection. Connecticut Historical Society, Hartford, Connecticut.

———. Letter to Lydia Huntley Sigourney dated September 3, 1841. Hoadly Collection. Connecticut Historical Society, Hartford, Connecticut.

Humphrey, Heman. *The Life and Labors of the Rev. T. H. Gallaudet, LL.D.* New York: Robert Carter, 1859.

Huntington, E. B. "Lydia H. Sigourney." In *Eminent Women of the Age: Being Narratives of the Lives and Deeds of the Most Prominent Women of the Present Generation*, 85–101. Hartford: S. M. Betts; Chicago: Gibbs & Nichols, 1869.

Huntley, Lydia H. *Moral Pieces in Prose and Verse.* Hartford, Conn.: Shelton and Goodwin, 1815.

Imbarrato, Susan Clair. *Traveling Women: Narrative Visions of Early America.* Athens: Ohio University Press, 2006.

"Interview of the Blind with the Deaf and Dumb." *Youth's Magazine*, April 14, 1837, 31.

Kelly, Gary. *Lydia Sigourney: Selected Poetry and Prose.* Petersborough, Canada: Broadview Press, 2008.

Knott, Sarah. *Sensibility and the American Revolution.* Chapel Hill: University of North Carolina Press, 2008.

Ladd, Paddy. *Understanding Deaf Culture: In Search of Deafhood.* Clevedon, U.K.: Multilingual Matters, 2003.

Lane, Harlan. *When the Mind Hears: A History of the Deaf.* New York: Vintage, 1989.

Leonard, Lynnette Grace. "A Rebel in Conservative Clothes: The Rhetorical Theory and Practice of Lydia Sigourney." PhD diss., University of Kansas, 2006.

Loew, Ruth C., C. T. Akamatsu, and Mary Lanaville. "A Two-Handed Manual Alphabet in the United States." In *The Signs of Language Revisited: An Anthology to Honor Ursula Bellugi and Edward Klima*, edited by Karen Emmorey and Harlan Lane, 245–59. Mahwah, N.J.: Erlbaum, 2000.

May, Caroline. *The American Female Poets: With Biographical and Critical Notices*. Philadelphia: Lindsay & Blakiston, [1848].

McGann, Jerome. *The Poetics of Sensibility: A Revolution in Literary Style*. Oxford: Clarendon Press, 1996.

"Note to 'La Sourde-Muette.'" *The Silent Worker* 4, no.36. (November 26, 1891): 1.

Okker, Patricia. "Sarah Josepha Hale, Lydia Sigourney, and the Poetic Tradition in Two Nineteenth-Century Women's Magazines." *American Periodicals* 3 (1993): 32–42.

Olwell, Victoria. "'It Spoke Itself': Women's Genius and Eccentric Politics." *American Literature* 77, no.1 (2005): 33–63.

Ostriker, Alicia Suskin. *Stealing the Language: The Emergence of Women's Poetry in America*. Boston: Beacon Press, 1986.

Parsons, Francis. *The Friendly Club and Other Portraits*. Hartford: Edwin Valentine Mitchell, 1922.

Patee, Fred Lewis. *The Feminine Fifties*. New York: Appleton, 1940.

Petrino, Elizabeth A. *Emily Dickinson and Her Contemporaries: Women's Verse in America, 1820–1885*. Hanover, N.H.: University Press of New England, 1998.

Phillips, Hiram. "Yale Teachers of the Deaf." *The Silent Worker* 14, no.7 (March 1902): 100.

"The Poets of America." Review of the *Poetical Works of Mrs. L. H. Sigourney* and three other books. *Irish Quarterly Review* 18 (June 1855): 193–220.

Robbins, Sarah. "'The Future Good and Great of our Land': Republican Mothers, Female Authors, and Domesticated Literacy in Antebellum New England." *The New England Quarterly* 75, no.4 (December 2002): 562–91.

Roller, Bert. "Early American Writers for Children: Lydia H. Sigourney." *Elementary English Review* 9 (1932): 233–34, 244, 248.

Root, Grace Cogswell. *Father and Daughter: A Collection of Cogswell Family Letters and Diaries (1772–1830)*. West Hartford: American School for the Deaf, 1924.

Sanborn, F. B. *Dr. S. G. Howe, the Philanthropist.* New York: Funk & Wagnalls, 1891.

Saunders, Richard, with Helen Raye. *Daniel Wadsworth, Patron of the Arts.* Hartford: Wadsworth Atheneum, 1981.

Sayers, Edna Edith, and Diana Gates. "Lydia Huntley Sigourney and the Beginnings of American Deaf Education in Hartford: It Takes a Village," *Sign Language Studies* 8, no.4 (2008): 369–411.

Searing, Laura Redden. Papers, 1846–1963. Western Missouri Historical Manuscript Collection, University of Missouri. Columbia, Missouri.

Sigourney, Lydia H. *Book for Girls.* New York: Turner & Hayden, 1844.

———. "Do Your Duty to Your Brothers and Sisters." *Youth's Magazine,* July 1837, 230–32.

———. "Essay on the Genius of Mrs. Hemans." In *The Works of Mrs. Hemans with a Memoir of her Life, and an Essay on Her Genius* by [Felicia] Hemans, Vol. 1, vii–xxvi. Philadelphia: Lea & Blanchard, 1840.

———. "Executive Committee of the Ladies for Greek Subscription Memorandum." Hoadly Collection. Connecticut Historical Society, Hartford, Connecticut.

———. "For Alice." Louis Balfour Papers. Gallaudet University Library Deaf Collections and Archives, Washington, D.C.

———. *The Girl's Reading-Book in Prose and Poetry for Schools.* New York: Clement & Packard, 1821.

———. *How to Be Happy.* Hartford: D. F. Robinson, 1833.

———. *Illustrated Poems.* Philadelphia: Carey & Hart, 1849; Lindsay & Blakiston, 1860.

———. Letter to the Ladies of the Directors of the American Asylum for the Education of the Deaf and Dumb. n.d.: draft letter pertaining to the August 18, 1821, organizational meeting. American School for the Deaf, Archives and Museum, West Hartford, Connecticut.

———. Letter to Seth Terry dated March 1, 1823. American School for the Deaf, Archives and Musuem, West Hartford, Connecticut.

———. Letter to Seth Terry dated January 1, 1828. American School for the Deaf, Archives and Musuem, West Hartford, Connecticut.

———. Letter to Laurent Clerc dated [n.d.,1836?] Eastman Collection. Gallaudet University Library Deaf Collections and Archives, Washington, D.C.

———. Letter to Laurent Clerc dated August 5, [1836?]. Eastman Collection. Gallaudet University Library Deaf Collections and Archives, Washington, D.C.

———. *Letters of Life.* New York: Arno, 1980. First published New York: Appleton, 1867.

———. *Letters to My Pupils*. 2nd ed. New York: Carter, 1856.

———. *Memoir of Phebe P. Hammond, a Pupil at the American Asylum at Hartford*. New York: Sleight & Van Norden, 1833.

———. "Minutes of the Society for the Former Scholars of Mrs. Sigourney." Lydia Huntley Sigourney Papers. Connecticut Historical Society Museum, Hartford, Connecticut.

———. *Olive Leaves*. New York: Robert Carter, 1852.

———. *Pocahontas, and Other Poems*. New York: Harper & Bros., 1841.

———. *Poems*. Boston: S. G. Goodrich: Boston, 1827; Hartford: H. J. Huntington, 1827.

———. *Poems*. Philadelphia: Key & Biddle, 1834.

———. *Poems*. New York: Leavitt & Allen [c.1841]; Philadelphia: John Locken, 1842 and 1844; Philadelphia: U. Hunt & Sons, 1846; New York: Leavett & Co., 1851; New York: Leavitt & Allen, 1853.

———. *Poetical Works of Lydia Howard Sigourney*, ed. F. W. N. Bayley. London: George Routledge & Co, 1850.

———. *Poetry for Children*. Hartford: Robinson & Pratt, 1834.

———. "Record of My School." Lydia Huntley Sigourney Papers. Connecticut Historical Society. Hartford, Connecticut.

———. *Sayings of the Little Ones*. Buffalo: Phinney, 1855; New York: Ivison & Phinney, 1858.

———. *Scenes in My Native Land*. Boston: James Munroe & Co., 1845; London: H. G. Clarke & Co., 1845.

———. *Select Poems*. 4th ed. Philadelphia: Frederick W. Greenough, 1838.

———. *Sketch of Connecticut, Forty Years Since*. Hartford: Oliver D. Cooke & Sons, 1824.

———. *Tales and Essays for Children*. Hartford: F. J. Huntington, 1835.

———. "To Fanny." Gilbert Eastman Collection. Gallaudet University Library Deaf Collections and Archives, Washington, D.C.

———. *The Western Home, and Other Poems*. Philadelphia: Parry & McMillan, 1854.

———. *Whisper to a Bride*. Hartford: H. S. Parsons & Co. 1850.

———. *Zinzendorff, and Other Poems*. New York: Leavitt, Lord & Co.; Boston: Crocker & Brewster, 1835, 1836, and 1837.

Strickland, Jane Margaret, ed. *Sacred Minstrelsy, or Poetry for the Devout*. London: Dean & Munday, 1838.

Teed, Melissa Ladd. "A Large Sphere of Usefulness: Women's Education and Public Life in Hartford, 1815–1850." *Connecticut History* 39, no.1 (2000): 1–22.

Tompkins, Jane. *Sensational Designs: The Cultural Work of American Fiction, 1790–1860*. New York: Oxford University Press, 1985.

Van Cleve, John V., and Barry A. Crouch. *A Place of Their Own: Creating the Deaf Community in America*. Washington, D.C.: Gallaudet University Press, 1989.

Wadsworth, Daniel. "Preface." In *Moral Pieces in Prose and Verse* by Lydia Huntley. Hartford: Sheldon & Goodwin, 1815. Unpaginated.

———. The Will of Daniel Wadsworth. Sterling Library. Yale University, New Haven, Connecticut, 1847.

Wainwright, J. M. "Intelligence and Remarks: Institution at Hartford for Instructing the Deaf and Dumb." *North American Review* 7 (1818): 127–36.

Wait, Gary E. "Lydia Huntley Sigourney and Deaf Education." *Dartmouth College Library Bulletin*, November 1992. http://www.dartmouth .edu/library/Library_Bulletin/Nov1992/LB-N92-Wait.html.

———. Personal correspondence to Diana Gates dated May 29, 2007.

Walker, Cheryl. *The Nightingale's Burden: Women Poets and American Culture Before 1900*. Bloomington: Indiana University Press, 1982.

Warren, Joyce W., ed. *The (Other) American Traditions: Nineteenth-Century Women Writers*. New Brunswick, N.J.: Rutgers University Press, 1993.

Washington, Augustus. "Letter to Lydia Sigourney, 8 July 1859." *African Repository* 35, no.16 (November 1859): 331–32.

Watts, Emily Stipes. *The Poetry of American Women from 1632 to 1945*. Austin: University of Texas Press, 1977.

Weld, Lewis. "The American Asylum." In *Tribute to Gallaudet*, by Henry Barnard, 131–50. Hartford: Brockett & Hutchinson, 1852. Adapted from "The American Asylum." *American Annals of the Deaf and Dumb* 1, no.1 (October 1847): 7–14.

Wood, Ann Douglas. "Mrs. Sigourney and the Sensibility of the Inner Space." *The New England Quarterly* 45, no.2 (1972): 163–81.

Wry, Joan R. "Lydia Sigourney's 'To a Shred of Linen': Lineaments of the Domestic and Sublime." *American Transcendental Quarterly* 22, no.2 (2008): 403–14.

"Young Lady 27 Years of Age: What I Thought of the Sun, Moon, and the Stars Before I Came to the Asylum." In *Eighth Report of the Directors of the American Asylum at Hartford for the Education and Instruction of the Deaf and Dumb*, 22. Hartford: W. Hudson & L. Skinner, 1824.

Zagarell, Sandra. "Expanding 'America': Lydia Sigourney's Sketch of Connecticut and Catherine Sedgewick's Hope Leslie." *Tulsa Studies in Women's Literature* 6, no.2 (1987): 225–45.

Index of First Lines